THE JOURNAL OF RISK AND INSURANCE

Volume 69, Number 1, March 2002

THE JOURNAL OF RISK AND INSURANCE

EDITORIAL POLICY

The Journal of Risk and Insurance publishes rigorous, original research in insurance economics and risk management. This includes the following areas of specialization: (1) industrial organization of insurance markets; (2) management of risks in the private and public sectors; (3) insurance finance, financial pricing, financial management; (4) economics of employee benefits, pension plans, and social insurance; (5) utility theory, demand for insurance, moral hazard, and adverse selection; (6) insurance regulation; (7) actuarial and statistical methodology; and (8) economics of insurance institutions. Both theoretical and empirical submissions are encouraged. Empirical work should provide tests of hypotheses based on sound theoretical foundations.

REVIEW PROCESS

The editors screen manuscripts submitted to *The Journal of Risk and Insurance* for suitability. Papers passing this initial screen are sent to referees. Based on the referee reports, the editor makes one of the following decisions: (1) accept, (2) accept subject to revisions, (3) return for major revisions and subsequent reconsideration, or (4) reject. The editor communicates the decision to the author(s) along with the referee reports.

Authorship of papers under consideration is anonymous to the reviewers, and the identities of reviewers are not revealed to the authors.

INDEXES

The Journal of Risk and Insurance is indexed by the American Economic Association's Economic Literature Index, the Finance Literature Index, the Social Sciences Citation Index, ABI/Inform, Business and Company ASAP, Lexis-Nexis, Dow Jones Interactive, and others.

COMMUNICATIONS

Communications relating to editorial matters should be addressed to Dr. Richard MacMinn, Editor, Attn: Ms. Kumi Smedley *Journal of Risk and Insurance*, MSIS Department, College of Business Administration, University of Texas, Austin, TX 78712. E-mail may be sent to the editor at jri1@uts.cc.utexas.edu. There is a $30 submission fee, which is waived for ARIA members. Checks must be payable to American Risk and Insurance Association. See the submissions instructions page on the Internet at the following address:

http://www.aria.org/jri/jristyle.html

For more information, contact the editor.

Books for review and book review submissions should be addressed to Dr. Norman A. Baglini, Book Review Editor, Department of Risk, Insurance, and Healthcare Management, Temple University, 485 Ritter Hall Annex 004-00, Philadelphia, PA 19122. E-mail: nbaglini@sbm.temple.edu or baglini@cpcuiia.org.

CONTENTS

ARIA
INSTITUTIONAL SPONSORS

PLATINUM SPONSORS

AMERICAN INSTITUTE FOR CPCU
GUS WORTHAM CHAIR IN RISK MANAGEMENT
  AND INSURANCE—UNIVERSITY OF TEXAS
  AT AUSTIN
SWISS RE CHAIR IN THE MANAGEMENT OF
  RISK—UNIVERSITY OF NOTTINGHAM
UNIVERSITY OF CALGARY

SILVER SPONSORS

ARTHUR ANDERSEN–GERMANY
TIAA-CREF

BRONZE SPONSORS

FARM BUREAU MUTUAL INSURANCE COMPANY
GRIFFITH FOUNDATION FOR INSURANCE
  EDUCATION
NATIONWIDE INSURANCE ENTERPRISE

FACULTY INTERNSHIP SPONSORS

CHUBB GROUP OF INSURANCE COMPANIES
THE CINCINNATI INSURANCE COMPANIES
ROYAL AND SUN ALLIANCE
SAFECO INSURANCE COMPANIES
THE ST. PAUL COMPANIES
STATE FARM MUTUAL INSURANCE COMPANIES
WESTFIELD COMPANIES

ARIA
ANNUAL MEETINGS

Dates and locations of the future annual
meetings of the American Risk and
Insurance Association are as follows:

MONTREAL

Hotel Omni Montreal

August 11-14, 2002

DENVER

Adam's Mark Hotel

August 10-13, 2003

CHICAGO

Westin Michigan Avenue Hotel

August 8-11, 2004

SALT LAKE CITY

Hilton Salt Lake City Hotel

August 7-10, 2005

WASHINGTON, D.C.

Capitol Hilton Hotel

August 6-9, 2006

©The Journal of Risk and Insurance, 2002, Vol. 69, No. 1, 1-7

Samuelson's Fallacy of Large Numbers and Optional Stopping

Erol A. Peköz

Abstract

Accepting a sequence of independent positive mean bets that are individually unacceptable is what Samuelson called a fallacy of large numbers. Recently, utility functions were characterized where this occurs rationally, and examples were given of utility functions where any finite number of good bets should never be accepted.[1] Here the author shows how things change if you are allowed the option to quit early: Subject to some mild conditions, you should essentially always accept a sufficiently long finite sequence of good bets. Interestingly, the strategy of quitting when you get ahead does not perform well, but quitting when you get behind does. This sheds some light on more possible behavioral reasons for Samuelson's fallacy, as well as strategies for handling a series of sequentially observed good investments.

Introduction and Overview

Samuelson (1963) told a story in which he offered a colleague a better than 50-50 chance of winning $200 or losing $100. The colleague rejected the bet, but said he would be willing to accept a string of 100 such bets. Samuelson argued that the colleague was irrationally applying the law of averages to a sum, and this perhaps has led to a more widely held perception that accepting a sequence of good bets when a single one would be rejected is a "fallacy of large numbers."

Since then a number of authors have studied this phenomenon. Samuelson (1989) gave examples of utility functions where a single bet is unacceptable but a sufficiently long finite sequence of good bets will be accepted. Also given were utility functions where a long sequence of good bets is never acceptable: Consider the utility function $U(x) = -2^{-x}$ and bets giving a 50 percent chance of losing $1 or winning $(1 + \epsilon)$, for a sufficiently small $\epsilon > 0$. It can be shown that expected utility decreases with each additional bet made, even though the bets are favorable and the utility function is increasing. Pratt and Zeckhauser (1987) studied the related property they labeled "proper risk aversion," where investors unwilling to make a single bet will also be unwilling to make more than one independent bet of the same type.

Erol Peköz is associate professor in the School of Management at Boston University. Thanks are due for helpful comments from Zvi Bodie, Stephen Ross, Paul Samuelson, and an anonymous referee.

[1] Ross, 1999.

Nielsen (1985) found necessary and sufficient conditions for a gambler with a concave utility function to eventually accept a sequence of bounded good bets, and Lippman and Mamer (1988) extended this to unbounded, identically distributed bets. Recently Ross (1999) extended this to independent but nonidentically distributed bets. The essential idea given in Lippman and Mamer (1988) and Ross (1999) is that if the utility function decreases faster than exponentially in the negative direction, the small risk of a loss can be magnified enough to overwhelm the benefits of a gain even for arbitrarily long sequences of good bets. Gollier (1996) gave some related results on how the availability of future optional bets can increase the attractiveness of a current bet, but the eventual attractiveness of a sufficiently large number of optional good bets has not been directly studied. See Bodie (1995) for a discussion of related phenomena surrounding long-term stock market investing.

Here the author shows what happens when the gambler has the option to quit early: A sufficiently long sequence of good bets should always be accepted, meaning that given a sequence of positive mean bets, for sufficiently large n you should always agree to sequentially make the first n of them with the option to quit early. This holds provided the gambler's utility function is not bounded from above, the expected utility of a single bet is finite, and a condition on the bet means and variances holds.

This result does not hold in the setting of Ross (1999) without a stopping option. There the total number of bets to be made is viewed as fixed in advance, while in the setting herein it is viewed as variable up to some maximum number that is fixed in advance. Note that the gambler is not allowed to play as long as it takes to get ahead, but is only allowed a maximum of n bets, which must be fixed in advance.

It is interesting to note that the strategy of quitting when you reach some large wealth level does not perform well. This is because even with arbitrarily long sequences of good bets, there can always be some small chance that the game ends with a very large loss, and a utility function can always be found that magnifies this loss more than enough to make the game unacceptable. One uses the strategy of quitting whenever the gambler's wealth goes below the starting wealth, and for sufficiently long sequences of good bets, the benefit of large gains always eventually overwhelms the risk of losses.

As a final note, much controversy exists over Samuelson's fallacy and the behavioral issues surrounding it. Benartzi and Thaler (1999), for example, used it as an example illustrating the limitations of expected utility theory in explaining behavior. This article shows that if faced with the opportunity to play a long sequence of favorable bets with the option to quit early, accepting the game is rational from an expected utility point of view.

The organization of the article is as follows. The next section contains the main result. The "Multiplicative Gambles" section has an analogous result for multiplicative payoffs. The "Summary" section summarizes the conclusions, and the "Appendix" section provides the proofs.

MAIN RESULT

Consider an infinite sequence of available bets, and let S_n be the wealth of a gambler who makes the first n bets. Ross (1999) defines a utility function U to have the Eventual

Acceptance Property (EAP) if

$$E[U(S_n)] > U(0) \quad \text{for some } n > 0,$$

meaning for some n the gambler will be willing to make the first n bets. Expanding on this notion, say that the utility function has the Eventual Acceptance with Stopping Option Property (EASOP) if

$$E[U(S_{T \wedge n})] > U(0) \quad \text{for some } n > 0 \text{ and stopping time } T,$$

where $x \wedge y$ denotes $\min(x,y)$, meaning that for some fixed n the gambler will be willing to make the first n bets with the option to stop early at any time, knowing the outcomes of all previous bets. Note that in the former case the gambler is required to agree to make all n bets in advance, whereas in the latter case the gambler agrees to make up to n sequential bets with the option to stop at any time along the way.

Here the concern is only with sequences of positive mean bets, which are represented as a sequence of independent random variables $X_1, X_2, \ldots$ with means μ_i satisfying $\mu = \inf_i \mu_i > 0$, and first let $S_n = \sum_{i=1}^{n} X_i$ denote the wealth of a gambler after the nth bet is made. Ross (1999) studied sequences of such positive mean bets and showed, subject to some additional side conditions, that the EAP holds if and only if a concave utility function, U, satisfies

$$\lim_{x \to -\infty} U(x)e^{\gamma x} \to 0$$

for all $\gamma > 0$. This type of condition was also previously given in Lippman and Mamer (1988, Theorem 4). The related side condition requiring finite bet variance is discussed in Lippman and Mamer (1988, Example 2).

More examples where the EAP does not hold can be easily created from this, such as when $U(x) = -e^{-x}$ on $(-\infty, 0)$ and is arbitrary above 0, preserving concavity. Letting, for example, $X_i \sim N(\frac{1}{4}, 1)$, a straightforward computation (see Ross, 1999), shows that the expected utility of the sequence S_n approaches $-\infty$ exponentially in n.

A consequence of the main result below is that the story is different for EASOP: With a sequence of good bets (and some side conditions), essentially all unbounded utility functions satisfy the EASOP. For sufficiently large n a gambler should always be willing to sequentially make the first n bets with the option to stop early. The author now formally states the main result.

Theorem 1. *Let $X_1, X_2, \ldots$ be a sequence of independent random variables with means μ_i and variances σ_i^2, and let the wealth after the nth bet be $S_n = \sum_{i=1}^{n} X_i$. Suppose*

$$\mu = \inf_i \mu_i > 0 \tag{1}$$

and

$$\sum_{i=1}^{\infty} \sigma_i^2 / i^2 < \infty. \tag{2}$$

If a utility function, U, satisfies

$$\lim_{x \to \infty} U(x) = \infty \tag{3}$$

and

$$\alpha = \inf_i E[U(X_i)] > -\infty, \tag{4}$$

then the EASOP holds.

Proof: See Appendix.

This means that, while for some utility functions it is rational to reject even an arbitrarily large number of sequential good bets, it is usually not rational if you have the option to quit early. This has implications for any sequentially observed investment situations—including, for example, investments made over a lifetime.

The intuition for the result is as follows. For the EAP not to hold, the utility function must decrease faster than an exponential function in the negative direction. This means that when losses are extremely costly, even with an arbitrarily long sequence of good bets the risk of incurring losses overwhelms the benefits of the gains. If early stopping is allowed, the gambler can always stop before losses get too severe, and this cuts the risk far enough to make a sufficiently long sequence of good bets attractive.

Note 1. Condition (2) is satisfied when there is a uniform bound on the variances; i.e., when

$$\sigma_i^2 \le \sigma, \ \forall i.$$

Note 2. For the proof, use the rule of stopping when wealth first goes below zero. Some condition like (2) is needed for this rule because if the variances increase too quickly, it may be too easy to go below zero even at high wealth levels. For example, suppose

$$U(x) = \begin{cases} \log_2 x & x > 0 \\ -10 & x < 0 \\ 0 & x = 0 \end{cases}$$

and

$$X_i = \begin{cases} +2^i & \text{with probability } 2/3 \\ -2^i & \text{with probability } 1/3. \end{cases}$$

In this case the rule will not work well. Starting with zero, it is easy to see that any time you lose a bet, your total wealth will be negative, and then expected utility equals

$$\log_2(2^{n+1} - 1)(2/3)^n - 10(1 - (2/3)^n),$$

which can be seen to be negative for all $n \ge 1$.

MULTIPLICATIVE GAMBLES

In many situations, gambles are multiplicative rather than additive. The same result as Theorem 1 essentially holds.

Theorem 2. *Let* $X_1, X_2, \ldots$ *be a sequence of independent random variables with* $\mu_i = E[\log(X_i)]$ *and* $\sigma^2 = \mathrm{Var}(\log(X_i))$, *and let the wealth after the nth bet be* $S_n = \prod_{i=1}^{n} X_i$. *Suppose* $\mu = \inf_i \mu_i > 0$ *and* $\sum_{i=1}^{\infty} \sigma_i^2 / i^2 < \infty$. *If a utility function,* U, *satisfies Equations* (3) *and* (4) *above, then the EASOP holds for any such sequence of multiplicative bets.*

Proof: See Appendix.

SUMMARY

While examples of utility functions exist in which very large numbers of good bets should not be accepted, no such utility functions exist if stopping early is allowed. A good stopping strategy for this turns out to be "quit while you're behind" rather than the perhaps more intuitive "quit while you're ahead." This is subject to the condition that utility functions are not bounded from above, any single bet has finite expected utility, and a mild condition on the payoff means and variances holds.

The author also mentions the idea that if someone given the option to make a sufficiently large number of good bets believes he or she has the option to stop early, accepting the game is rational. This may partly explain Samuelson's fallacy, the perception that a large sequence of good bets should always be accepted.

APPENDIX

Proof of Theorem 1: Without loss of generality, assume that the gambler starts at wealth level 0 with $U(0) = 0$. Define the stopping time T so that the gambler makes up to a total of n bets but will quit if the wealth ever goes below zero. Thus

$$T = n \wedge \min\{i \geq 1 : S_i < 0\},$$

where $x \wedge y$ denotes $\min(x, y)$. It will be shown that for sufficiently large n, $E[U(S_T)] > 0$ and hence the EASOP holds.

First, let

$$A = \{S_T > L\}$$

denote the event the gambler's wealth ends above L, for some fixed L. Compute the expected utility of the final wealth by conditioning using

$$E[U(S_T)] = E[U(S_T)|A]P(A) + E[U(S_T)|A^c]P(A^c), \tag{A1}$$

where A^c denotes the complement of A.

Use a slight generalization of the strong law of large numbers, which appears, for example, in Durrett (1996, p. 69, Exercise 8.4), stating that if $X_1, X_2, \ldots$ are independent mean 0 random variables satisfying condition (2) then $S_k / k \to 0$ as $k \to \infty$, where $\to$ denotes convergence with probability 1.

Applying this to the mean-zero variables $(X_i - \mu_i)$ obtains

$$(S_k - \sum_{i=1}^{k} \mu_i)/k \to 0$$

and thus

$$S_k/k \to \sum_{i=1}^{k} \mu_i/k \geq \mu,$$

which implies

$$\forall \epsilon > 0, \exists m : P(S_k \geq k\mu, \forall k > m) \geq 1 - \epsilon. \tag{A2}$$

Let $\epsilon = 1/2$ and use Equation (A2) to find an m so that

$$P(S_k \geq k\mu, \forall k > m) \geq 1/2. \tag{A3}$$

Using this choice of m, let

$$p = \frac{1}{2} \prod_{i=1}^{m} P(X_i \geq \mu), \tag{A4}$$

and note that $E[X_i] \geq \mu$ implies $p > 0$. Then by Equation (3), pick L sufficiently large so that

$$U(L) > -\alpha/p, \tag{A5}$$

and finally pick n sufficiently large so that $n > \max(m, L/\mu)$.

Now, because this choice of n gives $n\mu > L$,

$$\begin{aligned} P(A) &\geq P(S_n > L, S_k \geq k\mu, \forall k \geq 1) \\ &= P(S_k \geq k\mu, \forall k \geq 1) \\ &\geq P(B)P(C|B), \end{aligned}$$

where

$$B = \{X_k \geq \mu, \forall k : 1 \leq k \leq m\}$$

and

$$C = \{S_k \geq k\mu, \forall k > m\}.$$

A straightforward coupling argument gives $P(C|B) \geq P(C)$, and by Equation (A3), $P(C) \geq 1/2$. In addition, clearly $P(B) = 2p$, and combining these, $P(A) \geq p$.

Because U is nondecreasing in x, one must have $E[U(S_T)|A] \geq U(L)$, and condition (4) also gives $E[U(S_T)|A^c] \geq \alpha$. Thus by Equation (A1) we have

$$E[U(S_T)] \geq \alpha + U(L)p > 0, \tag{A6}$$

where the final inequality follows from the choice of L in Equation (A5). Note that for the first inequality of Equation (A6), assume $\alpha \leq 0$; otherwise the theorem would trivially hold with $T = 1$. This establishes the result. ∎

Proof of Theorem 2: Follows by applying Theorem 1 to the logarithms of the variables X_i. ∎

REFERENCES

Benartzi, S., and R. H. Thaler, 1999, Risk Aversion or Myopia? Choices in Repeated Gambles and Retirement Investments, *Management Science*, 45(3): 364-381.

Bodie, Z., 1995, On the Risk of Stocks in the Long Run, *Financial Analysts Journal*, 51(3): 18-22.

Durrett, R., 1996, *Probability: Theory and Examples*, 2nd ed. (Belmont, Calif: Wadsworth Publishing).

Gollier, C., 1996, Repeated Optional Gambles and Risk Aversion, *Management Science*, 42(11): 1524-1530.

Lippman, S. A., and J. W. Mamer, 1988, When Many Wrongs Make a Right, *Probability in the Engineering and Informational Sciences*, 2: 115-127.

Nielsen, L. T., 1985, Attractive Compounds of Unattractive Investments and Gambles, *Scandinavian Journal of Economics*, 87: 463-473.

Pratt, J. W., and R. J. Zeckhauser, 1987, Proper Risk Aversion, *Econometrica*, 55: 143-154.

Ross, S. A., 1999, Adding Risks: Samuelson's Fallacy of Large Numbers Revisited, *Journal of Financial and Quantitative Analysis*, 34(3): 323-339.

Samuelson, P., 1963, Risk and Uncertainty: A Fallacy of Large Numbers, *Scientia*, 98: 108-113.

Samuelson, P., 1989, The $\sqrt{N}$ Law and Repeated Risktaking, in: *Probability, Statistics, and Mathematics, Papers in Honor of Samuel Carlin* (Academic Press, Inc.), 291-306.

©*The Journal of Risk and Insurance*, 2002, Vol. 69, No. 1, 9-24

MORAL HAZARD, BASIS RISK, AND GAP INSURANCE

Neil A. Doherty
Andreas Richter

ABSTRACT

This article addresses the trade-off between moral hazard and basis risk. A decision maker, e.g., a primary insurer, is considered who can purchase an index hedge and a (re)insurance contract that covers the gap between actual losses and the index-linked payout, or part of this gap. The results suggest that combining insurance with an index hedge may extend the possibility set and by that means lead to efficiency gains. Naturally, the results depend heavily on the transaction costs associated with both instruments. In particular, the authors show that if the index product is without transaction costs, at least some index-linked coverage is always purchased, so long as there is positive correlation between the index and the actual losses. So under these circumstances, there is in any case a benefit from the availability of index products. Furthermore, it is shown that the index hedge would always be supplemented by a positive amount of gap insurance.

INTRODUCTION

An interesting recent development in capital markets has been the securitization of insurance risk. In many of these transactions, an insurance company hedges its exposure to earthquake or windstorm risk by means of some financial instrument that is held directly by investors. The most common structure is a bond[1] on which the principal or interest is forgiven if the natural hazard event occurs; thus the risk is passed

---

Neil Doherty is professor of insurance and risk management at the Wharton School, University of Pennsylvania. Andreas Richter is assistant professor of risk and insurance at the University of Hamburg, Germany. The authors would like to thank David Croson, Georges Dionne, Pierre Picard, and the participants of a finance colloquium at Goethe University, Frankfurt, for very helpful discussions. The input from two anonymous referees and the editor was also highly appreciated. Project support from an academic fellowship granted by the German Academic Exchange Service (DAAD) under the *Gemeinsames Hochschulsonderprogramm III von Bund und Ländern* is gratefully acknowledged.

[1] The transaction is normally fronted through a specially created entity, called a special purpose vehicle (SPV). The SPV reinsures the insurance firm and simultaneously issues the forgivable debt.

from the insurance company directly to the bondholders.[2] In 2000, these catastrophe bonds (CAT bonds) totaled $1.136 billion.[3] Another illustration is the catastrophe option created by the Chicago Board of Trade, although trade in such instruments seems to have been displaced by the emergence of the CAT bonds.

The rationale usually offered for such transactions is that the supply of the normal hedging instrument for insurers, i.e., reinsurance, is limited.[4] Thus, insurers who have a high exposure to losses through natural hazard have needed to replace or complement reinsurance by hedging directly with investors.

This explanation for insurance securitization is incomplete. While reinsurers were undoubtedly reluctant to offer much catastrophe reinsurance after Hurricane Andrew in 1992, their capacity clearly rose over the 1990s as more capital flowed into the industry, particularly into the Bermuda reinsurance market. Thus, one needs to explain what advantages might arise when insurance risk is transferred directly, rather than indirectly through holding reinsurance stocks. One explanation offered by Froot (1999) follows a market completeness line. By buying reinsurance shares, the investor acquires a residual stake in the portfolio of risks underwritten by the reinsurer and in its investment performance. Securitization offers investors the opportunity to take a pure position on the insured event. Thus, securitization unbundles insurance risk and expands the investor's opportunity set.[5,6]

A complementary explanation for securitization is that it has introduced a new contractual technology for addressing moral hazard. Moral hazard is present in all insurance transactions, including reinsurance. Primary insurers select a portfolio of risks to insure. Moreover, the primary negotiates the contract terms with its own policyholders, including what safety and loss reduction techniques should be required as a condition of insurance. When claims arise, the primary settles those claims with its policyholders. Each of these activities is costly to the primary insurer, yet each activity

---

[2] Other variations include contingent debt and equity financing. For example, the insurer issues put options on its own equity that can be triggered by the occurrence of the natural hazard. The occurrence of the event, together with the likely fall in the insurer's stock price, triggers the exercise of the put option. In this way, the insurer is able to recapitalize after the loss on terms fixed in advance. Moreover, since the put is exercised at less than the post-loss market price of equity, the loss is borne in part by the holders of the put option.

[3] See Laster and Raturi (2001) for details.

[4] See, e.g., Durrer (1996), Cholnoky, Zief, Werner, and Bradistilov (1998), Bantwal and Kunreuther (2000), and Cummins, Lalonde, and Phillips (2000).

[5] Other reasons may exist for securitization. For example, the placing of a debt forgiveness instrument in an SPV avoids the credit risk found in reinsurance contracts. As a reaction to this, some reinsurance structures have appeared that allocate individual contracts to "protected cells." This device avoids the prospect that poor performance on one contract could cause default on another. Each cell is effectively treated as a stand-alone firm.

[6] It may also be noted that such unbundling is hardly new. For example, Kohn (1999) described how early maritime financing contracts bundled a source of funding and an insurance policy. The development of early insurance markets was essentially an unbundling of these two instruments. Ironically, the point made here in the text is that part of the insurance risk can be transferred to capital markets to secure further unbundling. See also MacMinn (2000), who contrasted the developments described in Kohn's article with the recent convergence in finance and insurance.

can affect the frequency and severity of claims. If the primary is heavily reinsured, the reinsurer reaps the benefit of loss reduction but the cost is borne by the primary. To address this incentive conflict, reinsurance has contractual controls. As many principal agent conflicts are redressed through *ex post* settling up, reinsurance contracts may be experience rated or retrospectively priced. Thus, the reinsurance premium for any contract year would be influenced by the prior year's losses and can be further adjusted on a retrospective basis. Moreover, long-term and brokered relationships are common in reinsurance. This puts the primary insurer's reputation on the line, which further encourages it to undertake loss control.

Securitization has introduced a new set of contractual devices for addressing moral hazard that are now being used by insurers and reinsurers. In traditional reinsurance, one party (the primary insurer) owns an asset (its book of business) with a random value. A second asset, the reinsurance policy, is purchased, whose payoff is perfectly negatively correlated with the first. Thus, the reinsurance payout is a (usually simple) function of the primary insurer's own loss. In insurance language, it is an *indemnity* contract. In contrast, the payoff on many of the new hedging instruments used for insurance securitizations is not a function of the primary insurer's loss, but another random variable that has some correlation with that loss. For example, for securitizing earthquake risk, the triggering event is sometimes an index of the aggregated losses of all (or some sample of) insurers writing this risk, or more simply the location and Richter scale reading of the event. Similarly, an instrument securitizing hurricane risk might be triggered by the index of industry losses or more directly by the occurrence of a storm satisfying certain parameters (size, force, location, etc.).[7]

The use of such triggers involves a trade-off. On the one hand, the primary is not indemnified for its loss, so it is not a perfect hedge. There is some *basis risk*, which is the mismatch between the index and the primary's loss (basis risk is the inverse of, or some negative function of, the correlation coefficient). The quality of the hedge deteriorates as the correlation coefficient falls. On the other hand, there is an offsetting efficiency gain. The trigger for the instrument is largely outside the control of the primary insurer. For example, if the trigger is a loss index of many insurers, then the only control the primary has over the index is scaled to its share of the index. If it is not in the index, the primary has no influence on the index, and there is no moral hazard. Similarly, if the instrument is triggered by a hurricane's location and force, these parameters are not controlled by the primary insurer, and there is no moral hazard. In short, a trade-off exists between basis risk and moral hazard.

These nonindemnity triggers such as an industry index resemble *instrument variables* in that they are instruments that are correlated to the primary's portfolio but largely outside its control. The purpose of this article is to examine whether the use of such instrument variable contracts, either alone or in conjunction with indemnity contracts, leads to efficiency gains. The authors do this by allowing the one party, the policyholder (or the primary insurer in a reinsurance contract), to purchase a hedging vehicle based on an index or other instrument that is outside its control but still correlated to its own loss. This is referred to as an *index hedge*. If the correlation between the

---

[7] It is not necessary to securitize an insurance product to use an index trigger. Reinsurance may be sold by conventional reinsurers with such triggers. The point is that reinsurers have not relied on such controls, and they have in fact been popularized in CAT bonds and options.

instrument variable and the policyholder's loss is less than one, there is some basis risk. The policyholder can purchase a separate policy to cover the difference between its recovery on the instrument hedge and its own loss. This will be called *gap insurance*, although it is structurally similar to a *basis swap* used for interest rate transactions, a term that has also been used for such policies.[8] The moral hazard problem arises only from the gap insurance. The authors will examine how the risk-reward frontier is affected by this combination of hedge vehicles. In particular, it will be shown that indexed hedges avoid moral hazard associated with indemnity insurance. While purchasing the gap insurance reintroduces moral hazard, this also expands the opportunity set and permits the policyholder to achieve a preferred trade-off between risk transfer and moral hazard.

While the authors have introduced indexed products as an innovation by capital market players to avoid the moral hazard faced by reinsurance, this article is about contract structure, not about organization design. The combination of indexed hedges and gap insurance can be prepackaged in an insurance-linked security or in a reinsurance contract offered by a reinsurer. Indeed, insurers and reinsurers have become more active in recent years (possibly as a reaction to securitization) in providing new coverages and new policy triggers.

The article is organized as follows. The next section illustrates how recent insurance-linked securities have used innovative triggers. It will also show how the combination of index triggers and gap insurance resembles mutual insurance, and it will present a graphical comparison of index hedges and indemnity insurance under conditions of moral hazard. Then the authors will specify a model enabling the analysis of the joint use of an index hedge and gap insurance in a mean variance framework. The article concludes with a short summary, some remarks on limitations of this work, and ideas for future research.

INDEX HEDGE AND GAP INSURANCE

Insurance-Linked Securities

The use of industry indexes and other instrument variables to trigger insurance hedge products has become common in recent years.[9] In the early 1990s, the Chicago Board of Trade (CBOT) commenced trade in insurance option products, options written on an index of the underwriting results of a number of property-liability insurers doing business in regions of the United States with high risk of natural catastrophe. Insurers are natural holders of such options, and a limited volume of trade has occurred. The use of an index promotes liquidity, because instruments can be standardized. But it also provides some reassurance to investors that the trigger for exercising the option is largely beyond the control of insurers who take long positions. The CBOT options have now been largely eclipsed by a developing market in over-the-counter

---

[8] Basis swaps are often used to exchange different sets of floating interest rates. For example, a bank may have its assets and liabilities linked to two different interest indexes. Thus, while the assets and liabilities move in roughly the same direction, there is still basis risk. A swap transaction would permit the bank to hedge this basis risk. When used to hedge basis risk in this way, the basis swap fills a function identical to gap insurance as described here.

[9] For a more comprehensive overview of insurance-linked securities, see Belonsky, Laster, and Durbin (1999) or Laster and Raturi (2001).

insurance-linked securities.[10] These securities have been bond issues in which principal or interest is at risk, or they may have been swaps, contingent capital, or some form of convertible debt. The most active markets for such instruments are for natural catastrophes and weather risks.

While these securities are formally issued through special-purpose vehicles, the ultimate hedging party is normally an insurer or reinsurer. Insurers can use these vehicles to supplement or replace traditional reinsurance. But reinsurers have also made use of this market, usually to supplement their capital and expand the supply of traditional reinsurance. A recent exception to the use of this market by (re)insurers was a CAT bond issue designed to hedge the earthquake risk for the Tokyo Disney establishment. Some of these instruments use traditional indemnity triggers. For example, the CAT bond issues for USAA, an insurer of military personnel, were designed such that the debt would be forgiven in direct relationship to the losses of USAA. The failure to use an index for these issues is apparent when one looks at the book of business of this insurer. Since USAA's customers cluster around military bases, its loss experience from events such as hurricanes would not be representative of the insurance market as a whole. The correlation between the market index and this insurer's loss experience is low, and the index does not offer an effective hedge.

Other insurers have a spread of business that is more representative of the whole population, and their loss experience will match the overall industry loss experience more closely. For these insurers, the industry loss index offers an effective hedge against their own losses. The advantage of the index trigger is that it is difficult for the individual insurer to manipulate *ex post* if the hedging insurer's losses account for a small share of the index. Thus, the presence of an index hedge causes little dilution of the incentive of the insurer to control losses. There is little moral hazard. But such indexes do encounter other problems, primarily that the insurance losses often take a long time to settle, so the index may not be fully developed for a long time.

The third, more radical, type of trigger used in insurance-linked securities is the parametric trigger. The event is described by a set of technical parameters. For example, an earthquake has an energy reading (Richter scale), duration, and location, and the performance of the security is scaled directly to these parameters. The idea is that these parameters provide a rough predictor of the size of the claims faced by the insurer. This parametric trigger is even more immune from manipulation than the industry loss index and thereby addresses moral hazard. Moreover, it has the advantage over the index that the parameters can be determined very quickly.[11]

The Decomposition of Insurance Risk and Moral Hazard

The decomposition of insurance risk into idiosyncratic and diversifiable categories has been studied often. For example, Borch (1962, in an article that predates the capital

---

[10] See Laster and Raturi (2001) for recent market data.

[11] A further approach that is receiving attention is the modeled trigger. Here a computer model of the insurer's potential exposure to a whole range of potential losses is modeled and parameterized. When an actual event occurs, the model is rerun with the event parameters to determine a *predicted* amount of loss for the insurer. Insofar as the parameters of the model (though not of the particular event) have been fixed beforehand, the modeled trigger should also be safe from manipulation.

asset pricing model) showed that in a competitive market for insurance and other financial assets, entities will each hold the "market portfolio," and only nondiversifiable risk will be priced. In insurance terms, holding the market portfolio means fully insuring idiosyncratic risk but holding a participating policy in which each policyholder receives a risky dividend scaled to market loss experience.

This article is related to Smith and Stutzer (1995), who considered a decomposition of insurance coverage by means of participating policies to resolve moral hazard. However, the mechanism that generates this decomposition is very different from the one presented herein, and the resulting contract design is also different. It is well known that realized losses provide a signal of the policyholder's unobserved effort, and the sharing of those losses by the policyholder can be used to redress moral hazard. However, Holmström (1979) showed that when a second signal carries additional information on the agent's effort, the optimal contract will also use that signal.[12] Smith and Stutzer modeled an *ex post* moral hazard problem situation in which loss probabilities are determined by a policyholder action selected after a state of nature has been revealed. For example, a hurricane approaches the coast, and the policyholder must then decide on protective actions. Since the state of nature is an informative signal of the agent's effort, the optimal contract is conditioned on the state of nature. Smith and Stutzer contemplate states of nature that commonly expose groups of policyholders, so their optimal policy depends on the group loss as well as the idiosyncratic loss, i.e., a participating policy.

In contrast to Smith and Stutzer, the authors will address a moral hazard issue that can be *ex ante* or *ex post*. As in Smith and Stutzer's model, the insurance coverage will be conditioned upon both individual loss and a second random variable. However, the second trigger herein is selected for exactly the opposite reason as Smith and Stutzer's: because it is *noninformative* of the agent's action. In contrast, the second trigger is selected only because it is correlated with the loss.

Define some instrument, I, called an index, which is correlated with the policyholder's loss, L, but over which the policyholder has little or no control. Contingent payments, based upon this index, can be purchased. Let α denote the hedge ratio; thus the payout from this product is αI. Also define the gap, G, as the difference between L and this payout.

$$G = L - \alpha I \quad \text{where} \quad 0 \le r_{I,L} \le 1 \tag{1}$$

($r_{I,L}$ denotes the correlation coefficient).

With a simple *indemnity insurance* contract, the policyholder insures the loss, L, so the contract payoff is defined solely on L. The problem addressed here is to permit the

---

[12] Holmström's article looks at the use of additional triggers that are selected because they carry additional information on the agent's hidden action. These signals are described as "informative." This article looks at additional triggers that carry little or no information on the action (are noninformative) but are simply correlated with the loss. Thus, this case is orthogonal to Holmström. A further comparison of Holmström's informative signals with noninformative index triggers is given in Doherty and Mahul (2001), who showed that Holmström's model can be expanded to include noninformative index triggers.

party at risk to hedge or insure I and G separately. The hedging tools are referred to as *index hedge* and *gap insurance*. If the hedge ratio for the gap, meaning the fraction (β) of G that is covered through gap insurance, is unity, then the combination of index and gap insurance will form a perfect hedge, or full insurance. However, varying the hedge ratios α and β offers different controls of moral hazard to a simple indemnity contract in which L is hedged directly. Specifically, it is shown that separate hedges on the index and the gap expand the risk-return opportunity set available to the policyholder and can provide an efficiency gain.

The use of instruments such as industry indexes to control moral hazard has been raised by several writers. Doherty (1997) used a simple model to point out the trade-off between basis risk and moral hazard, and Croson and Kunreuther (2000) classified the different instruments (including insurance and financial instruments) used by insurers to manage catastrophe risk according to a performance criterion including the control of moral hazard (see also Froot, 1999). None of these articles has formally modeled this problem and addressed whether the introduction of an index hedge offers efficiency gains compared with simple indemnity contracts.[13] The authors will address this trade-off in a simple principal agent model in which a policyholder is able to purchase both an index hedge and gap insurance.

Contrasting an Indemnity Policy and an Index Hedge

The idea of index policies and moral hazard is illustrated in Figure 1 in mean standard deviation space (W denotes the policyholder's wealth). A conventional indemnity policy is first illustrated. Starting at endowment point S, an indemnity policy might be purchased covering a portion β of the exposure at a premium of $P(\beta)$. Since moral hazard exists, the premium will increase at an increasing rate as more insurance is purchased.[14] Indemnity coverage is $\beta = 0$ at S, and $\beta = 1$ at D. The line shows the usual trade-off between risk sharing and efficiency. The optimal point is shown at the tangency of the opportunity line and an indifference curve.

Now consider an index hedge. The index is some instrument variable that is correlated with the loss but over which the policyholder has little or no control. Examples given in the introduction included an aggregate of all insurer losses or a parametric description of some event such as an earthquake or hurricane. An index hedge will not encounter moral hazard if the index is independent of the policyholder's action a. But the basis risk from an index hedge depends on the correlation between the index and the policyholder's loss. At a very high correlation, and under the assumption that there is no transaction cost, then a point such as A might be reached. Notice that with the index contract, the attainable frontier is SA, as opposed to SD under the conventional insurance policy. The index frontier SA therefore dominates the indemnity insurance frontier over at least part of its range. At a lower correlation, a hedge point B might be reached that, although it has higher risk than the optimal insurance, is still preferred to the insurance. The reason for the preference is that the increase in

---

[13] See, however, Nell and Richter (2000) for a formal model that addresses the trade-off between transaction cost and basis risk.

[14] See, for example, Holmström (1979). Note in Figure 1 that, as coverage and the premium increase, one moves from S toward D. The increasing downward slope moving left indicates the increasing premium rate.

FIGURE 1

Index Hedge and Insurance

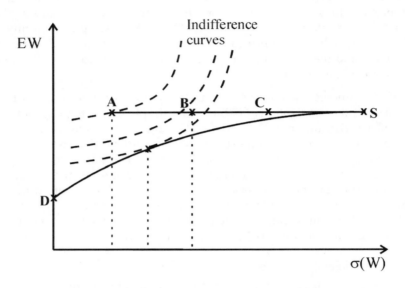

expected wealth from resolving moral hazard more than compensates for the increase in risk. Finally, at a lower correlation, the index product can only deliver a wealth prospect such as C, which is inferior to the indemnity insurance.

JOINT PURCHASE OF AN INDEX HEDGE AND GAP INSURANCE

Model Specification and Basic Results

The index hedge offers a payout of αI in return for a premium of $(1 + m)\alpha EI$ (here and in the following, E denotes the expectation of a stochastic variable). The term m is a transaction cost incurred by the insurer who, being risk neutral, is indifferent about selling coverage at this price or not doing so. The gap coverage pays some proportion of the basis risk left from the index hedge, i.e., $\beta(L - \alpha I)$, in exchange for a premium of $\beta\{EL(a) - \alpha EI + n\}$. The loading ($\beta n$) is assumed to depend only on the level of coverage since the expected payments from the gap insurance may be close to zero.[15] Note that when $\alpha = 0$ an indemnity policy exists with coverage $\alpha I + \beta(L - \alpha I) = \beta L$.

The loss distribution depends on the level of loss prevention carried out by the policyholder (a, which formally is the expenditure on loss prevention). It will be specified later precisely how loss prevention affects the distribution, but for the moment it is noted that the main effect is a reduction of the expected value of the loss: $EL(a)$, with $EL_a < 0, EL_{aa} > 0$. This model is sufficiently general to allow for actions that affect

---

[15] To illustrate this point, notice that $\beta(L - \alpha I)$ can be either positive or negative and may be close to zero. Thus, to adopt the usual modeling practice of setting the premium loading as a function of the expected coverage will lead to strange results. Given the upside and downside nature of the gap insurance, it makes more sense to set the loading as a function of the coverage parameter, β.

either the size or probability of loss and can be used to address both *ex ante* and *ex post* moral hazard.

In setting the problem, one wishes to be able to identify the optimal contract given moral hazard. The insurer is assumed to be risk neutral and the insurance market to be competitive such that insurers charge a premium just sufficient to cover expected claims (which, in turn, depends on the anticipated action a^* and other transaction costs). The optimal contract is identified by allowing the policyholder a choice of hedge ratios at these quoted premiums and a subsequent choice of action on safety.[16]

The wealth of the policyholder, W, is now (W_0 denotes the initial wealth)

$$W = W_0 - L - (1 + m)\alpha EI - \beta\{EL(a^*) - \alpha EI + n\} + \alpha I + \beta(L - \alpha I) - a$$
$$= W_0 - L(1 - \beta) + I\alpha(1 - \beta) + EI\alpha(\beta - 1 - m) - EL(a^*)\beta - \beta n - a. \qquad (2)$$

The decision maker considered is a firm whose value is increasing in EW. Moreover, since the firm has certain costs (bankruptcy costs, agency costs, etc.) that increase with risk, the firm value is decreasing in $\sigma^2(W)$.[17] The use of mean variance has several advantages here. First, the main actors in this market are firms, not individuals, and mean variance fits well with much of the corporate finance literature. Second, a critical feature of this model is the relationship between the index, I, and the policyholder's loss, L, and mean variance analysis allows simple comparative statics on the correlation coefficient. Mean variance does permit one to derive rich results, although these are restricted in application. A particular limitation of mean variance analysis is its inability to capture the properties of long-tail distributions, which describe many corporate risks.[18]

$$EW = W_0 - \beta EL(a^*) - (1 - \beta)EL(a) - mEI\alpha - \beta n - a \text{ and} \qquad (3)$$
$$\sigma^2(W) = \sigma^2(L)(1 - \beta)^2 + \sigma^2(I)\alpha^2(1 - \beta)^2 - 2\alpha(1 - \beta)^2 COV(I; L)$$
$$= (1 - \beta)^2\{\sigma^2(L) + \alpha^2\sigma^2(I) - 2\alpha COV(I; L)\}. \qquad (4)$$

Firm value is mean variance where λ is a measure of the risk associated costs:

$$V = EW - \lambda\sigma^2(W). \qquad (5)$$

---

[16] As with other principal agent problems, the insurance moral hazard problem trades off risk sharing and efficiency. It makes no difference formally whether the risk sharing is defined by the coverage function in the policy or by retroactively adjusting premiums to loss experience.

[17] See, for example, Doherty and Tinic (1981), Mayers and Smith (1982), Stultz (1984), Shapiro and Titman (1985), Doherty (1985), Froot, Scharfstein, and Stein (1993), and Nance, Smith, and Smithson (1993).

[18] The combination of assuming a risk-neutral insurer and a risk-averse policyholder is not unusual and probably has relatively little effect on the qualitative results. More generally, one could assume a risk-averse policyholder and a less risk-averse insurer (which leave room for gains from trade in risk transfer). This is not likely to add sufficient additional insight to warrant the complexity.

Ex post choice of a,

$$-(1 - \beta)\frac{dEL(a)}{da} - 1 - \lambda(1 - \beta)^2 \left[\frac{d\sigma^2(L)}{da} - 2\alpha\frac{dCOV(I;L)}{da}\right] = 0. \qquad (6)$$

The optimal insurance problem is

$$MAX_{\alpha,\beta,a} \; EW - \lambda\sigma^2(W) \quad \text{s.t. condition (6) (with } \Omega \text{ as the multiplier)} \qquad (7)$$

yielding the first-order conditions (α^*, β^*, a^* denote the optimal solution)

$$-mEI - 2\lambda(1 - \beta^*)^2 \left[\alpha^*\sigma^2(I) - COV(I;L) - \Omega\frac{dCOV(I;L)}{da}\right] = 0 \qquad (8)$$

and

$$\Omega\frac{dEL(a^*)}{da} - n + 2\lambda(1 - \beta^*)$$
$$\left[\sigma^2(L) + \alpha^{*2}\sigma^2(I) - 2\alpha^*COV(I;L) + \Omega\frac{d\sigma^2(L)}{da} - 2\alpha^*\Omega\frac{dCOV(I;L)}{da}\right] = 0. \qquad (9)$$

One can simplify things by assuming that the safety function has the following properties:

$$\frac{dEL}{da} < 0, \quad \frac{d^2EL}{da^2} > 0, \quad \frac{d\sigma^2(L)}{da} = 0, \quad \frac{dCOV(I;L)}{da} = 0. \qquad (10)$$

Thus, Equation (8) can be restated in closed form (noting that $COV(I;L) = r_{I,L}\sigma(I)\sigma(L)$) as

$$\alpha^* = r_{I,L}\frac{\sigma(L)}{\sigma(I)} - \frac{mEI}{2\lambda(1 - \beta^*)^2\sigma^2(I)} \qquad (8')$$

and Equation (9) can also be restated in closed form as

$$\beta^* = 1 + \frac{\Omega\frac{dEL(a^*)}{da} - n}{2\lambda[\sigma^2(L) + \alpha^{*2}\sigma^2(I) - 2\alpha^*r_{I,L}\sigma(I)\sigma(L)]}. \qquad (9')$$

The comparative statics are mostly straightforward. The optimal co-share on the index coverage, α^*, is positively related to $r_{I,L}$, $\sigma(L)$ and the risk-aversion parameter λ, and it is negatively related to m and EI. The role of $\sigma(I)$ is unclear if there are transaction costs. If the index coverage is without transaction cost, $m = 0$ (and if, of course, there is positive correlation between L and I), then the firm will hedge at some positive hedge ratio, $\alpha^* > 0$, which depends on the correlation coefficient and the ratio of the standard deviation of the loss to the standard deviation of the index. But with a transaction cost, $m > 0$, the optimal hedge ratio depends on the optimal gap insurance, β^*.

The optimal gap coverage, β^*, is equal to 1 (giving a full indemnity coverage) if there is no moral hazard, $dEL/da = 0$, and there is no premium loading, $n = 0$. Further, β^* falls as moral hazard increases,[19] and it is positively related to λ.

Observe the relationship between α^* and β^*:

$$\frac{d\beta^*}{d\alpha^*} = \frac{\left(\Omega\frac{dEL(a)}{da} - n\right)\left(r_{I,L}\sigma(I)\sigma(L) - \alpha^*\sigma^2(I)\right)}{\lambda\left(\sigma^2(L) + \alpha^{*2}\sigma^2(I) - 2\alpha^*r_{I,L}\sigma(I)\sigma(L)\right)^2}. \tag{11}$$

Since λ is positive and the first term in parentheses in the numerator is negative, the sign of $d\beta^*/d\alpha^*$ depends on the various risk terms in the final parentheses in the numerator. It can be shown that

$$\frac{d\beta^*}{d\alpha^*} < 0 \quad \text{i.f.f.} \quad r_{I,L}\sigma(L) > \alpha^*\sigma(I) \quad \text{and} \tag{12}$$

$$\frac{d\beta^*}{d\alpha^*} > 0 \quad \text{i.f.f.} \quad r_{I,L}\sigma(L) < \alpha^*\sigma(I). \tag{13}$$

As it stands, a high correlation leads to a negative relationship between α^* and β^*. This result is fairly plausible: If the index hedge is highly effective, it is likely that the less gap insurance is needed, the more coverage from the index hedge is purchased.[20]

Competitive Market—No Transaction Costs

When $m = n = 0$, the result is quite transparent. Equations (8') and (9') can be restated as

$$\alpha^* = r_{I,L}\frac{\sigma(L)}{\sigma(I)} \quad \text{and} \tag{8''}$$

$$\beta^* = 1 + \frac{\Omega\frac{dEL(a^*)}{da}}{2\lambda[\sigma^2(L) + \alpha^{*2}\sigma^2(I) - 2\alpha^*r_{I,L}\sigma(I)\sigma(L)]}. \tag{9''}$$

Substituting Equation (8'') into Equation (9'') gives

$$\beta^* = 1 + \frac{\Omega\frac{dEL(a^*)}{da}}{2\lambda\sigma^2(L)(1 - r_{I,L}^2)}. \tag{14}$$

One can interpret the optimal index hedge, α^*, and the optimal gap insurance, β^*, for this simplified case. Equation (8'') shows that, as was mentioned above, α^* is increasing in the correlation coefficient, $r_{I,L}$, at a slope that depends on the relative values of $\sigma(L)$

---

[19] β^* is positively related to dEL/da, but since this is negative, β^* falls the more sensitive EL is to changes in a.

[20] Note, however, that the righthand side in the condition in Equations (12) and (13) increases in α^*.

and $\sigma(I)$. However, with a transaction cost, $m > 0$, the index hedge ratio is shifted down (see Equation (8')).

With no moral hazard, β^* is unity. But with moral hazard, β^* is less than unity and declines with the correlation coefficient, as shown in Equation (14). With zero correlation, the optimal coverage is $1 + \{\Omega dEL(a^*)/da\}/\{2\lambda\sigma^2(L)\}$. As the correlation increases, β^* will decline as the second term in Equation (9'') gets smaller (recall that this term is negative). The firm will, however, always purchase a positive amount of gap insurance. The following proposition summarizes features of the optimal solution.

Proposition: *If no transaction costs exist ($m = n = 0$), and under the assumptions stated in Equation (10), the optimal coverage from the index hedge, α^*, is positive if $r_{I,L} > 0$ and increases in $r_{I,L}$. The optimal gap insurance policy always offers positive, but less than full, coverage ($0 < \beta^* < 1$).*

Proof: See Appendix.

To make intuitive sense out of these results, consider Figure 2. Starting with an initial endowment at point S, an index coverage is available with no moral hazard, which can take the decision maker to point B if there is low correlation or to point A if there is higher correlation. The risk gap, AC or BC (depending on the correlation), can be insured with the gap coverage. This gives an opportunity locus of either AD (if high correlation) or BD (if low correlation). Either way, insuring the gap gives rise to moral hazard and will lead to the common risk-return point D if the full gap is insured. Take the low-correlation case first. With zero loading, $m = 0$, the index coverage will be independent of the gap coverage, as shown by Equation (8''). If only an index coverage is purchased, the firm will be at position B on indifference curve I(4). Since the risk is high, the indifference curve is relatively steep at B. But gap coverage can be bought along the line BD. Since the slope of this line is zero at position B and thus

FIGURE 2

Combining Index and Gap Coverage

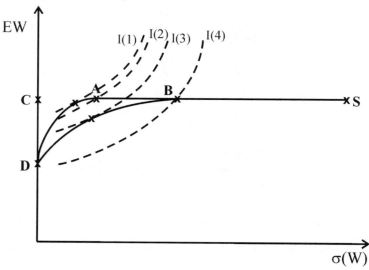

flatter than the indifference curve I(4), the firm benefits from taking gap coverage to attain indifference curve I(3). Thus $0 < \beta^* < 1$. But with high correlation, the firm can attain position A on indifference curve I(2) with index coverage alone. Only little gap coverage is bought that leads to indifference curve I(1).

Transaction Costs

The above-mentioned case with transaction costs is now illustrated. Figure 3 shows possible combinations of index and gap coverage for this situation. Position A, as in Figure 2, shows a risk-return position attainable with just an index hedge, assuming quite high correlation between the index and the firm's loss. Transaction costs to the index hedge shift the opportunity line from SA down to SA'. In addition to the moral hazard costs, the gap coverage has other transaction costs (the difference between D and D' is a measure of transaction costs at full coverage). In the situation shown here, the new optimal hedge combination is point F, where some gap coverage is purchased. A' is dominated by certain combinations of both hedging tools, particularly along the line $A''F$. As was shown formally in Equation (8'), less index coverage is bought in comparison to the case without transaction costs. However, other results are possible depending on the relative values of the transaction costs for the index and gap coverages.

CONCLUSION

The goal of this article was to analyze risk-sharing efficiency effects due to the use of index-linked instruments and particularly the joint use of these tools and indemnity insurance. For that purpose, in contrast to the existing literature on the demand for index-linked risk-sharing devices, the problem was formalized. The authors considered the risk management decision of a firm, e.g., a primary insurer, who has the following options for covering risk: First, an index hedge may be purchased, i.e., a type

FIGURE 3
Index and Gap Coverage With Transaction Costs

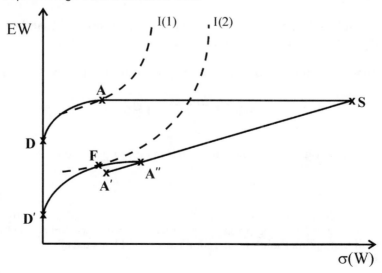

of coverage based upon an instrument variable such as a catastrophe index, which is largely out of the policyholder's control and thus would not, or at least not to a significant extent, be affected by moral hazard. The downside of this kind of instrument would usually be that it cannot be a perfect hedge or that, in other words, the decision maker would have to face basis risk. So to possibly reduce this problem, the authors introduced as an additional hedging tool the opportunity of a (re)insurance contract that covers the gap between actual losses and the index hedge.

This insurance contract is again subject to moral hazard.[21] The authors showed, however, that combining insurance with an index hedge might extend the possibility set and by that means lead to efficiency gains. This becomes especially instructive for the case in which the index product is without transaction costs: Under these circumstances the firm always buys at least some index-linked coverage, if the index is positively correlated with its actual loss. Moreover, the index hedge would always be supplemented by a positive amount of gap insurance. So in any case, compared to the sole use of indemnity insurance, a benefit exists from combining index products and gap insurance.

The problem was tackled in a mean variance framework. An interesting extension of this work might be to discuss the usefulness of index hedge and gap insurance as a means to reduce moral hazard in an expected utility context. Furthermore, the authors simplified the model by assuming that the insured's effort does not affect the correlation between index and actual losses. Thus, an important task for future research will be to generalize this analysis by allowing this kind of interaction. Changing the model in this way will certainly complicate things drastically, although dramatic changes of result structure are not expected.

APPENDIX

Proposition: *If no transaction costs exist ($m = n = 0$), and under the assumptions stated in Equation (10), the optimal coverage from the index hedge, α^*, is positive if $r_{I,L} > 0$ and increases in $r_{I,L}$. The optimal gap insurance policy always offers positive, but less than full, coverage ($0 < \beta^* < 1$).*

Proof: To complete the proof, show only that $\beta^* > 0$, by showing that the slope of the gap insurance opportunity locus is zero, where $\beta = 0$.

First, note that under the assumptions of the proposition, Equation (6) simplifies to

$$-(1 - \beta)\frac{dEL(a)}{da} - 1 = 0. \tag{6'}$$

This defines a function $a(\beta)$. Furthermore, there is (see Equation (4))

$$\sigma^2(W) = (1 - \beta)^2\sigma^2(G), \tag{A1}$$

---

[21] And, of course, full coverage—assuming no difference in price—yields exactly the same moral hazard problems as full coverage from simple indemnity insurance. But note at first the well-known result that optimal solutions to moral hazard problems usually include coinsurance or deductibles.

where $\sigma^2(G) = \sigma^2(L) + \alpha^2\sigma^2(I) - 2\alpha COV(I; L)$.

This yields $\beta = 1 - \frac{\sigma(W)}{\sigma(G)}$.

Now see that $EW = EW(a(\beta(\sigma^2(W))))$. Thus we get

$$\frac{dEW}{d(\sigma(W))} = \frac{dEW}{da} \cdot \frac{da}{d\beta} \cdot \frac{d\beta}{d(\sigma(W))}. \tag{A2}$$

From Equation (6'), it follows that this expression is equal to zero for $\beta = 0$.

Finally, if $\frac{dEW}{d(\sigma(W))} = 0$ at $\beta = 0$, then $\beta = 0$ cannot be an optimum for any risk-averse agent, because the slope of the opportunity set must equal the agent's marginal rate of substitution between risk and return. Thus, a risk-averse agent would choose some positive gap insurance.   ■

REFERENCES

Bantwal, V. J., and H. C. Kunreuther, 2000, A Cat Bond Premium Puzzle?, *Journal of Psychology and Financial Markets*, 1: 76-91.

Belonsky, G., D. S. Laster, and D. Durbin, 1999, *Insurance-Linked Securities* (Zurich: Swiss Re).

Borch, K., 1962, Equilibrium in a Reinsurance Market, *Econometrica*, 30: 424-444.

Cholnoky, T. V., J. H. Zief, E. A. Werner, and R. S. Bradistilov, 1998, *Securitization of Insurance Risk—A New Frontier*, Goldman Sachs Investment Research.

Croson, D. C., and H. C. Kunreuther, 2000, Customizing Indemnity Contracts and Indexed Cat Bonds for Natural Hazard Risks, *Journal of Risk Finance*, 1: 24-41.

Cummins, J. D., D. Lalonde, and R. D. Phillips, 2000, The Basis Risk of Catastrophic-Loss Index Securities, Working paper 00-22-B-B (Philadelphia: Financial Institutions Center, The Wharton School, University of Pennsylvania).

Doherty, N. A., 1985, *Corporate Risk Management: A Financial Exposition* (New York: McGraw-Hill).

Doherty, N. A., 1997, Financial Innovation for Financing and Hedging Catastrophe Risk, in: N. R. Britton and J. Oliver, eds., *Financial Risk Management for Natural Catastrophes*, Proceedings of a conference sponsored by Aon Group Australia Limited (Brisbane: Griffith University), 191-209.

Doherty, N. A., and O. Mahul, 2001, Mickey Mouse and Moral Hazard: Uninformative but Correlated Triggers, Working paper (Philadelphia: The Wharton School, University of Pennsylvania).

Doherty, N. A., and S. M. Tinic, 1981, A Note on Reinsurance Under Conditions of Capital Market Equilibrium: *Journal of Finance*, 36: 949-953.

Durrer, A., ed., 1996, Insurance Derivatives and Securitization: New Hedging Perspectives for the US Catastrophe Insurance Market, *sigma* no. 5 (Zurich: Swiss Re).

Froot, K. A., 1999, The Evolving Market for Catastrophic Event Risk, *Risk Management and Insurance Review*, 3: 1-28.

Froot, K. A., D. S. Scharfstein, and J. C. Stein, 1993, Risk Management: Coordinating Corporate Investment and Financing Policies, *Journal of Finance*, 48: 1629-1658.

Holmström, B., 1979, Moral Hazard and Observability, *Bell Journal of Economics*, 10: 74-91.

Kohn, M., 1999, Risk Instruments in the Medieval and Early Modern Economy, *Working Paper 99-07* (Hanover, NH: Dartmouth College).

Laster, D., and M. Raturi, 2001, Capital Market Innovation in the Insurance Industry, *sigma* no. 3 (Zurich: Swiss Re).

MacMinn, R., 2000, Risk and Choice: A Perspective on the Integration of Finance and Insurance, *Risk Management and Insurance Review*, 3: 69-79.

Mayers, D., and C. W. Smith Jr., 1982, On the Corporate Demand for Insurance, *Journal of Business*, 55: 281-296.

Nance, D. R., C. W. Smith Jr., and C. W. Smithson, 1993, On the Determinants of Corporate Hedging, *Journal of Finance*, 48: 267-284.

Nell, M., and A. Richter, 2000, Catastrophe Index-Linked Securities and Reinsurance as Substitutes, Working paper no. 56, Working Paper Series: Finance and Accounting (Frankfurt: Johann Wolfgang Goethe-University).

Shapiro, A. C., and S. Titman, 1985, An Integrated Approach to Corporate Risk Management, *Midland Corporate Finance Journal*, 3: 41-56.

Smith, B. D., and M. Stutzer, 1995, A Theory of Mutual Formation and Moral Hazard With Evidence From the History of the Insurance Industry, *The Review of Financial Studies*, 8: 545-577.

Stultz, R., 1984, Optimal Hedging Policies, *Journal of Financial and Quantitative Analysis*, 19: 127-140.

©The Journal of Risk and Insurance, 2002, Vol. 69, No. 1, 25-44

PRICING DEFAULT-RISKY CAT BONDS WITH MORAL HAZARD AND BASIS RISK

Jin-Ping Lee
Min-Teh Yu

ABSTRACT

This article develops a contingent claim model to price a default-risky, catastrophe-linked bond. This model incorporates stochastic interest rates and more generic loss processes and allows for practical considerations of moral hazard, basis risk, and default risk. The authors compute default-free and default-risky CAT bond prices by using the Monte Carlo method. The results show that both moral hazard and basis risk drive down the bond prices substantially; these effects should not be ignored in pricing the CAT bonds. The authors also show how the bond prices are related to catastrophe occurrence intensity, loss volatility, trigger level, the issuing firm's capital position, debt structure, and interest rate uncertainty.

INTRODUCTION

Property-liability insurance companies traditionally hedge their low-loss frequency, high-loss-severity catastrophe risks by buying catastrophe reinsurance contracts. The traditional reinsurance and catastrophe insurance options, which trade in the Chicago Board of Trade (CBOT), are asset hedge instruments for insurers' or reinsurers' catastrophe risk management. A recent innovation in catastrophe risk management is the catastrophe bond (CAT bond, hereafter). The CAT bond, which is also named as an "Act of God bond" or "insurance-linked bond," is a liability hedge instrument for insurance companies, for which there have been many successful CAT bond issues recently.[1] CAT bond provisions have debt-forgiveness triggers whose generic design allows for the payment of interest and/or the return of principal forgiveness, and the extent of forgiveness can be total, partial, or scaled to the size of loss. Moreover, the debt forgiveness can be triggered by the insurer's (or reinsurer's) actual losses or on a composite index of insurers' losses during a specific period.

Jin-Ping Lee is from Chaoyang University of Technology, Wufon, Taichung, Taiwan. Min-Teh Yu is from Yuan Ze University, Jung-Li, Taiwan. The authors are grateful for the referees and seminar participants at the Taiwan Finance Association Annual Meeting and the Financial Management Association Annual Meeting for valuable comments, and to the National Science Council of Taiwan for financial support.
[1] See American Academy of Actuaries (1999).

The advantage of a CAT bond hedge for (re)insurers (insurers, hereafter) is that the issuer can avoid the credit risk that may arise with traditional reinsurance or catastrophe-linked options. The CAT bondholders provide the hedge to the insurer by forgiving existing debt. Thus, the value of this hedge is independent of the bondholders' assets, and the issuer has no risk of nondelivery on the hedge. However, from the bondholder's perspective, the default risk, the potential moral hazard behavior, and the basis risk of the issuing firm are critical in determining the value of CAT bonds.

The moral hazard behavior occurs when the insurer's cost of loss control efforts exceeds the benefits from debt forgiveness. That is, the insurer has an incentive to pay the claims more generously when the loss amount is near the trigger set in the debt-forgiveness provision. Doherty (1997) pointed out that moral hazard results from less loss control efforts by the insurer issuing CAT bonds because these efforts will increase the amount of debt that must be repaid. Bantwal and Kunreuther (1999) also noted the tendency for insurers to write additional policies in a catastrophe-prone area, spending less time and money in their auditing of losses after a disaster. The moral hazard behavior may increase the claim payments at the expense of the bondholders' coupon (or principal) reduction and affect the bond price.

Another important element that needs to be considered in pricing a CAT bond is the basis risk. The CAT bond's basis risk refers to the gap between the insurer's actual loss and the composite index of losses that prevents the insurer from receiving complete risk hedging. The basis risk may cause insurers to default on their debt in the case of high individual loss but low index of loss, and therefore affects the bond price. A trade-off indeed exists between basis risk and moral hazard. If one uses an independently calculated index to define the CAT bond payments, then the insurer's opportunity to cheat the bondholders is reduced or eliminated, but basis risk is created. Doherty (1997) and Belonsky (1998), among others, have looked into the effect of basis risk and moral hazard, but not from the perspective of bond pricing.[2]

Only a few articles focus on the pricing of catastrophe-linked securities. For example, Cox and Schwebach (1992), Cummins and Geman (1995), and Chang, Chang, and Yu (1996) priced the CAT futures and CAT call spreads under the condition of deterministic interest rate and specific property claims services (PCS) loss processes. Litzenberger, Beaglehole, and Reynolds (1996) priced a one-year zero-coupon CAT bond and compared the CAT bond price calculated by the bootstrap approach with that estimated by hypothetical catastrophe loss distribution. Zajdenweber (1998) followed Litzenberger, Beaglehole, and Reynolds (1996) but changed the catastrophe loss distribution to the stable Levy distribution. Loubergé, Kellezi, and Gilli (1999) numerically estimated the CAT bond price under the assumptions that the catastrophe loss follows a pure Poisson process, the loss severity is an independently identical lognormal distribution, and the interest rate is driven by a binomial random process.

Most of these pricing models fail to incorporate a commonly acceptable stochastic interest rate process and catastrophe loss process and do not look into the default risk of the CAT bond. This study intends to contribute to the literature by setting up a new

---

[2] Canter, Cole, and Sandor (1997) and Laurenzano (1998) introduced the restriction and potential of the new catastrophe-linked securities, while Davidson (1998) and Bouzouita and Young (1998) focused on the regulations or applications from the perspective of risk management.

framework to fill this gap and to value the bond under the practical considerations of default risk, moral hazard, and basis risk. The rest of the article is organized as follows. The following section presents the asset, interest rate, and loss dynamics for a model of insurers. The next section specifies the payoffs of CAT bonds under various scenarios and values the CAT bonds. The subsequent section provides the numerical analysis and discusses the results, and the conclusion follows.

A Model for CAT Bond Issuers

CAT bonds can be issued by a traditional insurer or through a special purpose company (SPC) that is set up to issue CAT bonds. The specification here of an asset and liability structure can fit both types of issuers. The authors assume that it is a traditional insurer throughout the article, because it allows one to investigate how the issuing firm's capital position and debt structure will affect the price of CAT bonds. The issuer can be viewed as an SPC by redefining its assets and liabilities and using a different set of parameter values for them. This section first specifies the asset, interest rate, and aggregate loss dynamics and then shows their corresponding processes under the risk-neutralized pricing measure.

The Asset Dynamics

The typical way to model asset dynamics assumes a lognormal diffusion process for the asset value; for example, as in Merton (1977) and Cummins (1988). The main disadvantage of this modeling approach is that it fails to take into account the explicit impact of stochastic interest rates on the asset value. This is important for modeling the insurer's asset value, because it is quite common for insurers to hold a large proportion of fixed-income assets in their portfolios. In particular, insurers that issue CAT bonds mainly invest their proceeds from CAT bond sales in high-grade, interest-rate-sensitive investments such as commercial papers and treasury securities.

To measure the effect of the interest rate risk on CAT bond prices, we adopt the approach of Duan, Moreau, and Sealey (1995) to describe the insurer's total asset value as consisting of two risk components: interest rate and credit risk. The term *credit risk* refers to all risks that are orthogonal to the interest rate risk. Specifically, the value of an insurer's assets is governed by the following process:

$$\frac{dA_t}{A_t} = \mu_A dt + \phi dr_t + \sigma_A dW_{A,t},$$ (1)

where A_t is the value of the insurer's total assets at time t; r_t is the instantaneous interest rate at time t; $W_{A,t}$ is the Wiener process that denotes the credit risk; μ_A is the instantaneous drift due to the credit risk; σ_A is the volatility of the credit risk; and ϕ is the instantaneous interest rate elasticity of the insurer's assets.

The instantaneous interest rate is assumed to follow the square-root process of Cox, Ingersoll, and Ross (1985). This setting avoids the negative interest rate that may appear in Vasicek's model (1977). The instantaneous interest process can be written as

$$dr_t = \kappa(m - r_t)dt + v\sqrt{r_t}dZ_t,$$ (2)

where κ is the mean-reverting force measurement; m is the long-run mean of the interest rate; v is the volatility parameter for the interest rate; and Z_t is a Wiener process independent of $W_{A,t}$. Combining Equations (1) and (2), the asset dynamics can be described as follows:

$$\frac{dA_t}{A_t} = (\mu_A + \phi\kappa m - \phi\kappa r_t)dt + \phi v \sqrt{r_t}dZ_t + \sigma_A dW_{A,t}. \tag{3}$$

For derivative pricing, it is standard to use the device of risk neutralization. The dynamics for the interest process under the risk-neutralized pricing measure, denoted by Q, can be written as

$$dr_t = \kappa^*(m^* - r_t)dt + v \sqrt{r_t}dZ_t^*, \tag{4}$$

where κ^*, m^*, and Z_t^* are defined as

$$\kappa^* = \kappa + \lambda_r$$

$$m^* = \frac{\kappa m}{\kappa + \lambda_r}$$

$$dZ_t^* = dZ_t + \frac{\lambda_r \sqrt{r_t}}{v}dt.$$

The term λ_r is the market price of interest rate risk and is a constant under Cox, Ingersoll, and Ross (1985); Z_t^* is a Wiener process under Q.[3] The insurer's asset dynamics can be risk neutralized to

$$\frac{dA_t}{A_t} = r_t dt + \phi v \sqrt{r_t}dZ_t^* + \sigma_A dW_t^*, \tag{5}$$

where W_t^* is a Wiener process under Q and is independent of Z_t^*.

Aggregate Loss Dynamics
Follow the typical setting for loss dynamics in the actuarial literature (see Bowers, Gerber, Hickman, Jones, and Nesbitt, 1986) and model the aggregate loss as a compound Poisson process, a sum of jumps. Let $C_{i,t}$ represent the aggregate loss for issuing firm i and, to estimate the impact of basis risks on the CAT bond price, $C_{index,t}$ represents that for a composite index of losses (e.g., a PCS index). These two processes can be described as follows:

$$C_{i,t} = \sum_{j=1}^{N(t)} X_{i,j}, \tag{6}$$

and

$$C_{index,t} = \sum_{j=1}^{N(t)} X_{index,j}, \tag{7}$$

where the process $\{N(t)\}_{t\geq 0}$ is the loss number process, which is assumed to be driven by a Poisson process with intensity λ. Terms $X_{i,j}$ and $X_{index,j}$ denote the amount of losses caused by the jth catastrophe during the specific period for the issuing insurance company and the composite index of losses, respectively. Terms $X_{i,j}$ ($X_{index,j}$), for $j = 1,2,\ldots,N(T)$, are assumed to be mutually independent, identical, and lognormally distributed variables that are also independent of the loss number process, and their

---

[3] A presentation of the formula can also be found in Ritchken (1996, p. 552).

logarithmic means and variances are μ_i (μ_{index}) and σ_i^2 (σ_{index}^2), respectively. In addition, assume that the correlation coefficients of the logarithms of $X_{i,j}$ and $X_{index,j}$, for $j = 1,2,\ldots,N(T)$, are equal to ρ_x.

For valuation purposes, one needs to know the loss dynamics under the risk-neutralized pricing measure Q. When the loss process has jumps, the market is incomplete, and there is no unique pricing measure. Thus, follow Merton (1976) and assume that the overall economy is only marginally influenced by localized catastrophes such as earthquakes and hurricanes, and that the loss number process, $\{N(t)\}_{t \geq 0}$, and the amount of losses, $X_{i,j}$ and $X_{index,j}$, pertain to idiosyncratic shocks to the capital markets. The catastrophic shocks will represent "nonsystematic" risk and have a zero risk premium. By assuming that such a jump risk is nonsystematic and diversifiable, attaching a risk premium to this risk is unnecessary. This assumption is important, because one cannot apply a risk-neutral valuation to situations in which the size of the jump is systematic. For a discussion of this point, see Naik and Lee (1990), Cummins and Geman (1995), and Cox and Pedersen (2000). The aggregate loss processes, Equations (6) and (7), thus retain their original distributional characteristics after changing from the physical probability measure to the risk-neutralized pricing measure.

PRICING CAT BONDS

Once the risk-neutral processes of asset, loss, and interest rate dynamics are known, one can value the CAT bond price by the discounted expectation of its various payoffs in the risk-neutral world. The authors specify the payoffs of the CAT bonds under alternative considerations in this section. The authors first present the basic case, in which there is no default risk, and then look into the default-risky CAT bonds with potential basis risk and moral hazard.

Default-Free CAT bonds

Consider a hypothetical CAT discount bond[4] whose payoffs (PO_T) at maturity (i.e., time T) are as follows:

$$PO_T = \begin{cases} a * L & \text{if } C_T \leq K \\ rp * a * L & \text{if } C_T > K, \end{cases} \tag{8}$$

where K is the trigger level set in the CAT bond provisions; C_T is the aggregate loss at maturity; rp is the portion of the principal needed to be paid to bondholders when the forgiveness trigger has been pulled; L is the face amount of the issuing firm's total debts, which includes the face amount of the CAT bond; and a is the ratio of the CAT bond's face amount to total outstanding debts.

To price the CAT bond with the payoffs specified in Equation (8), assume the state variables are composed of θ and η, which determine that the term structure of interest rate and the aggregate loss are sufficiently well behaved to be able to apply the risk-neutral approach of Cox and Ross (1976) and Harrison and Pliska (1981). More specifically, under the risk-neutralized pricing measure Q, the CAT bond price on the

---

[4] Most CAT bonds in the market are one-year bonds without interim coupon payments. One can extend this model to price coupon-paying bonds by treating them as a portfolio of zero-coupon bonds with different maturities.

issuing date (i.e., time 0) can be written as follows:

$$P_{CAT}(0) = E^*_{\theta,\eta}[e^{-\int_0^T r_s ds} PO_T],$$ (9)

where $P_{CAT}(0)$ is the CAT bond price at time 0 and $E^*_{\theta,\eta}$ denotes expectations in a risk-neutral world.

It is reasonable to further assume that the state variables constituting θ, which for the purpose of valuing catastrophe risk bonds are essentially the term structure of interest rates, are independent of the state variables constituting η, which relate to catastrophe risk variables. The CAT bond price then becomes

$$P_{CAT}(0) = E^*_{\theta}\left[e^{-\int_0^T r_s ds}\right] E^*_{\eta}[PO_T],$$ (10)

where $E^*_{\theta}[e^{-\int_0^T r_s ds}]$ is the risk-free bond, and its solution, which can be found in Cox, Ingersoll, and Ross (1985), is desnoted as $B_{CIR}(0,T)$. In addition, $E^*_{\eta}[PO_T]$ can be written as $a*L*Pr[C_T \leq K] + rp*a*L*Pr[C_T > K]$, where $Pr[C_T \leq K]$ denotes the probability of the aggregate loss not being larger than the trigger level K. One can now present the CAT bond price as follows:

$$P_{CAT}(0) = B_{CIR}(0,T) * \left[\sum_{j=0}^{\infty} e^{-\lambda T}\frac{(\lambda T)^j}{j!}F^j(K) + rp(1 - \sum_{j=0}^{\infty} e^{-\lambda T}\frac{(\lambda T)^j}{j!}F^j(K)\right],$$ (11)

where

$$F^j(K) = Pr(X_{i,1} + X_{i,2} + \cdots + X_{i,j} \leq K)$$

denotes the jth convolution of F, and

$$B_{CIR}(0,T) = A(0,T)e^{-B(0,T)r},$$

where

$$A(0,T) = \left[\frac{2\gamma e^{(\kappa+\gamma)\frac{T}{2}}}{(\kappa + \gamma)(e^{\gamma T} - 1) + 2\gamma}\right]^{\frac{2\kappa m}{v^2}}$$

$$B(0,T) = \frac{2(e^{\gamma T} - 1)}{(\gamma + \kappa)(e^{\gamma T} - 1) + 2\gamma}$$

$$\gamma = \sqrt{\kappa^2 + 2v^2}.$$

Approximating an Analytical Solution. Under the assumption that the catastrophe loss amount is independent and identically lognormally distributed, the exact distribution of the aggregate loss at maturity, denoted as $f(C_T)$, cannot be known. However, to set up an approximating analytical solution, approximate the exact distribution by a lognormal distribution, denoted as $g(C_T)$, with specified moments. Jarrow and Rudd (1982), Turnbull and Wakeman (1991), and Nielson and Sandmann (1996) used the same assumption in approximating the values of Asian options and basket options.

Following the same approach, one only needs to set the first two moments of $g(C_T)$ to be equal to those of $f(C_T)$, which can be written as

$$\mu_g = E[C_T] = \lambda T e^{\mu_i + \frac{1}{2}\sigma_i^2} \tag{12}$$

$$\sigma_g^2 = Var[C_T] = \lambda T e^{2\mu_i + 2\sigma_i^2}, \tag{13}$$

where μ_g and σ_g^2 denote the mean and variance of the approximating distribution $g(C_T)$, respectively.

The value of the CAT bond can be shown as follows:

$$B_{app}(0) = B_{CIR}(0,T) \left[\int_0^K \frac{1}{\sqrt{2\pi}\sigma_g C_T} e^{-\frac{1}{2}(\ln C_T - \mu_g)^2} dC_T + rp \int_K^\infty \frac{1}{\sqrt{2\pi}\sigma_g C_T} e^{-\frac{1}{2}(\ln C_T - \mu_g)^2} dC_T \right], \tag{14}$$

where $B_{app}(0)$ is the approximating analytical CAT bond price at time 0. This formula is similar to Litzenberger, Beaglehole, and Reynolds (1996), except that they used a constant interest rate in the model. The authors will compare the analytical solution estimates and estimates from the numerical method without the approximating assumption in the Numerical Analysis section.

Default-Risky CAT bonds

The assumption of no default in the previous section is for the derivation of CAT bonds' analytical presentation. In this section, the authors look into the practical considerations of default risk, basis risk, and moral hazard relating to CAT bonds, specify their payoffs, and then value them using the numerical method in the next section.

When the insurer becomes insolvent and defaults, assume that the CAT bondholders have priority for salvage over the other debtholders because the proceeds from CAT bond sales are usually invested in a trust fund and can be liquidated only for the purpose of paying limited claims or returning to the bondholders. If the insurer is solvent, then CAT bondholders can receive the full principal of CAT bonds when the underlying losses are lower than the trigger level; otherwise, they can be repaid only part of the principal.

The authors first specify the default-risky payoffs when there is no basis risk; i.e., the insurer's debt is forgiven when its actual loss is larger than a specific amount of loss. The authors then compare the payoffs with those having a basis risk in which the debt is forgiven on some composite index of losses. At the end of this section, the authors present a framework to model the moral hazard behavior.

No Basis Risk. Basis risk refers to the risk that the losses that individual insurers incur will not have an anticipated correlation with the underlying loss index of the CAT bond. Basis risk might reduce the hedging effect of CAT bonds and increase the default probability of the issuing firm. In the case of no basis risk, the default-risky payoffs of CAT bonds can be written as follows:

$$
PO_{i,T} = \begin{cases} a * L & \text{if } C_{i,T} \leq K \text{ and } C_{i,T} \leq A_{i,T} - a * L \\ rp * a * L & \text{if } K < C_{i,T} \leq A_{i,T} - rp * a * L \\ Max\left\{A_{i,T} - C_{i,T}, 0\right\} & \text{otherwise,} \end{cases} \tag{15}
$$

where $PO_{i,T}$ are the payoffs at maturity for the CAT bond forgiven on the issuing firm's own actual losses; $A_{i,T}$ is the issuing firm's asset value at maturity; $C_{i,T}$ is the issuing firm's aggregate loss at maturity; and L, a, K, and rp are defined as in the previous sections.

With Basis Risk. In the case of the CAT bond being forgiven on the composite index of losses, the default-risky payoffs can be written as follows:

$$
PO_{index,T} = \begin{cases} a * L & \text{if } C_{index,T} \leq K \text{ and } C_{i,T} \leq A_{i,T} - a * L \\ rp * a * L & \text{if } C_{index,T} > K \text{ and } C_{i,T} \leq A_{i,T} - rp * a * L \\ Max\left\{A_{i,T} - C_{i,T}, 0\right\} & \text{otherwise,} \end{cases} \tag{16}
$$

where $C_{index,T}$ is the value of the composite index at maturity, and a, L, rp, $A_{i,T}$, $C_{i,T}$, and K are the same as defined in Equation (15).

According to the payoff structures of these CAT bonds and the specified asset and interest rate dynamics, the CAT bonds can be valued as follows:

$$
P_i(0) = \frac{1}{a * L} E_0^*[e^{-\bar{r}T} PO_{i,T}] \tag{17}
$$

$$
P_{index}(0) = \frac{1}{a * L} E_0^*[e^{-\bar{r}T} PO_{index,T}], \tag{18}
$$

where $P_i(0)$ is the default-risky CAT bond price with no basis risk; $P_{index}(0)$ is the default-risky CAT bond price with basis risk at time 0; E_0^* denotes expectations taken on the issuing date under pricing measure Q; $\bar{r}$ is the average risk-free interest rate between the issuing date and maturity date; and $\frac{1}{a*L}$ is used to normalize the CAT bond prices for a face amount of one dollar.

Moral Hazard. Moral hazard may need to be taken into account when the CAT bond is forgiven on the issuing firm's own losses, because the issuing firm has an incentive to settle claims more generously when the loss incurred approaches the trigger level. In this model, assume that the issuing firm relaxes its settlement policy once the accumulated losses fall into the range close to the trigger. This would then cause an increase in expected losses for the next catastrophe. Specify the change in the loss process as follows:

$$
\mu_i' = \begin{cases} (1 + \alpha)\mu_i & \text{if } (1 - \beta)K \leq C_{i,j} \leq K, \\ \mu_i & \text{otherwise,} \end{cases} \tag{19}
$$

where μ_i' is the logarithmic mean of the losses incurred by the $(j + 1)$th catastrophe when the accumulated loss $C_{i,j}$ falls in the specified range, $(1 - \beta)K \leq C_{i,j} \leq K$; α is a positive constant, reflecting the percentage increase in the mean; and β is a positive constant that specifies the range of moral hazard behavior.[5]

The analytical framework is fully specified. The authors do not expect a closed-form solution for such a complex contingent contract and therefore estimate CAT bond prices by numerical analysis in the next section.

NUMERICAL ANALYSIS

This section estimates the prices of CAT bonds using the Monte Carlo method. The authors establish a set of parameters and base values that are summarized in Table 1, while deviations from the base values are set to assess the comparative effect of these parameters on CAT bond prices. For simplicity, assume that the total amount of the issuing firm's debts, which include CAT bonds, has a face value of $100 and that the maturity of the CAT bond is equal to one year. The simulations are run on a weekly basis with 20,000 paths.

The initial asset/liability (or capital) position (A/L) ratios are set to be 1.1, 1.2, and 1.3, respectively. The average A/L ratio for the insurance industry has been about 1.3 on a book-value basis over the past ten years. The interest rate elasticity of the insurer's assets is set at 0, –3, and –5, respectively, to measure how the insurer's interest rate risk affects CAT bond prices. The volatility of the asset return that is caused by the credit risk is set to be 5 percent. The initial spot interest rate and the long-run interest rate are both set at 5 percent. The mean-reverting force is set to be 0.2, while the volatility of the interest rate is set at 10 percent. The market prices of interest rate risk are set at 0 and –0.01, respectively. These term structure parameters are all within the ranges typically used in the previous literature.

The occurrence intensities of catastrophe losses are set to be 0.5, 1, and 2, respectively, to reflect the frequencies of catastrophe events per year. Also assume the parameter values for catastrophe loss to be the same for individual insurers and the composite loss index. Set the logarithmic mean, μ_i and μ_{index}, to be 2, and the logarithmic standard deviations, σ_i and σ_{index}, to be 0.5, 1, and 2. Having different values for the index and individual insurers can be done without further difficulties, but it increases the dimension of calculation and does not provide more insights to this analysis of basis risks. The analysis will focus on the coefficient of correlation between the individual loss and the loss index, ρ_x, rather than on their means and standard deviations. The portion of principal needed to be repaid, rp, is set at 0.5 when debt forgiveness has been triggered. The ratio of the amount of CAT bonds to the insurer's total debt, a, is set to be 0.1. In addition, three different trigger levels (K) are set at 100, 110, and 120.

The authors now compute the default-free CAT bond prices using the numerical method and the approximating solution. Table 2 reports the bond prices under alternative sets of occurrence intensities and loss variances. Observe that the values of the approximating solution and the values from the numerical method are very close and within the range of ten basis points for most cases. The differences do not change

---

[5] This approach to moral hazard is *ad hoc*, but the authors do not know of any other articles incorporating this feature. The authors would like to view it as a first step and hope that it may inspire others to take up the challenge of modeling moral hazard.

TABLE 1
Parameter Definitions and Base Values

Asset Parameters		Values
A	insurer's assets	A/L ratios: 1.1, 1.2, and 1.3
μ_A	drift due to credit risk	
ϕ	interest rate elasticity of asset	0, –3, –5
σ_A	volatility of credit risk	5%
W_A	Wiener process for credit shock	
Interest Rate Parameters		
r	initial instantaneous interest rate	5%
κ	magnitude of mean-reverting force	0.2
m	long-run mean of interest rate	5%
v	volatility of interest rate	10%
λ_r	market price of interest rate risk	0, –0.01
Z	Wiener process for interest rate shock	
Catastrophe Loss Parameters		
μ_i	mean of the logarithm of the amount of catastrophe losses for the insurer	2
μ_{index}	mean of the logarithm of the amount of catastrophe losses for the composite loss index	2
σ_i	standard deviation of the logarithm of the amount of catastrophe losses for the insurer	0.5, 1, 2
σ_{index}	standard deviation of the logarithm of the amount of catastrophe losses for the composite loss index	0.5, 1, 2
ρ_x	correlation coefficient of the logarithms of amounts of catastrophe losses of the insurer and the composite index	0.5, 0.8, 1
$N(t)$	Poisson process for the occurrence of catastrophes	
Other Parameters		
K	trigger levels	100, 110, 120
rp	the ratio of principal needed to be paid if debt forgiveness is triggered	0.5
a	the ratio of the amount of CAT bond to total debts	0.1
α	moral hazard intensity	20%
β	the ratio set below the trigger that will bring about the insurer's moral hazard	20%
L	the total amount of insurer's debts	100

TABLE 2

Default-Free CAT bond Prices: Approximating Solution vs. Numerical Estimates No Moral Hazard and Basis Risk

	Approximating Solutions			Numerical Estimates					
				$\lambda_r = 0$			$\lambda_r = -0.01$		
				Triggers					
(λ, σ_i)	100	110	120	100	110	120	100	110	120
(0.5,0.5)	0.95112	0.95117	0.95120	0.95126	0.95126	0.95126	0.95119	0.95119	0.95119
(0.5,1)	0.94981	0.95009	0.95031	0.94988	0.95017	0.95040	0.94977	0.95029	0.95062
(0,5,2)	0.92933	0.93128	0.93293	0.92805	0.92952	0.93152	0.92675	0.92903	0.93103
(1,0.5)	0.95095	0.95106	0.95113	0.95126	0.95126	0.95126	0.95119	0.95119	0.95119
(1,1)	0.94750	0.94829	0.94887	0.94689	0.94822	0.94869	0.94825	0.97877	0.94977
(1,2)	0.90559	0.90933	0.91254	0.90270	0.90660	0.90955	0.90273	0.90682	0.91058
(2,0.5)	0.95038	0.95071	0.95091	0.95121	0.95126	0.95126	0.95110	0.95115	0.95119
(2,1)	0.94015	0.94259	0.94441	0.94070	0.94346	0.94546	0.93916	0.94263	0.94492
(2,2)	0.85939	0.86603	0.87183	0.85156	0.85846	0.86446	0.85065	0.85717	0.86378

All estimates are computed using 20,000 simulation runs. Bond prices are per face amount of one dollar.

much if the market price of interest rate risk changes from 0 to -0.01.[6] In addition, the approximate CAT bond prices are higher than those estimated by the Monte Carlo simulations for a high value of σ_i. This is because the approximate lognormal distribution underestimates the tail probability of losses, and this underestimation will be more significant when the loss standard deviation (σ_i) is high. Note also that the CAT bond price increases with trigger levels and that this increment rises with occurrence intensity and loss variance. For example, in the case where the occurrence intensity (λ) is 2 and the loss standard deviation (σ_i) is 2, the CAT bond prices will increase 65–69 basis points when the trigger level increases from 100 to 110, while the CAT bond prices will increase 60–66 basis points when the trigger level increases from 110 to 120.

Table 3 reports the prices of the default-risky bond and the effect of moral hazard under alternative values of initial capital position (A/L), catastrophe intensity, loss variance, and interest rate elasticity of the issuing firm's assets. The three (upper, middle, lower) values reported in each cell of Table 3 represent the corresponding estimate under the interest rate elasticity of 0, –3, and –5, respectively. A higher (absolute) value of interest rate elasticity corresponds to higher asset volatility and default risk of the issuer. Thus, one would expect the upper value of each cell (the CAT bond price for $\phi = -0$) to be higher than the middle and lower values (the CAT bond price for $\phi = -5$).

As is also expected, the higher the initial capital position (A/L) of the issuing firm, the lower the default risk and the higher the CAT bond prices. The increment of price changes increases with occurrence intensity and catastrophe loss volatility. One can

---

[6] Hereafter, the authors only report the bond prices calculated when the market price of interest rate risk is –0.01. Bond prices when the market price of interest rate risk is 0 are available from the authors.

TABLE 3

Default-Risky CAT bond Prices With Moral Hazard ($\lambda_r = -0.01$)

(λ, σ_i)	A/L = 1.1			A/L = 1.2			A/L = 1.3		
				Triggers					
	100	110	120	100	110	120	100	110	120
				No Moral Hazard					
(0.5,0.5)	0.95119	0.95119	0.95119	0.95119	0.95119	0.95119	0.95119	0.95119	0.95119
	0.95119	0.95119	0.95119	0.95119	0.95119	0.95119	0.95119	0.95119	0.95119
	0.95119	0.95119	0.95119	0.95119	0.95119	0.95119	0.95119	0.95119	0.95119
(0.5,1)	0.94891	0.94919	0.94924	0.94926	0.94968	0.95002	0.94940	0.94993	0.95021
	0.94864	0.94898	0.94898	0.94910	0.94958	0.94963	0.94931	0.94984	0.95998
	0.94847	0.94876	0.97876	0.94896	0.94944	0.94953	0.94977	0.95029	0.95062
(0.5,2)	0.90510	0.90619	0.90633	0.90693	0.90903	0.91045	0.90828	0.91056	0.91237
	0.90490	0.90633	0.90666	0.90702	0.92903	0.93103	0.90845	0.91069	0.91240
	0.90443	0.90572	0.90605	0.90680	0.90870	0.90975	0.90791	0.90991	0.91148
(1,0.5)	0.95119	0.95119	0.95119	0.95119	0.95119	0.95119	0.95119	0.95119	0.95119
	0.95119	0.95119	0.95119	0.95119	0.95119	0.95119	0.95119	0.95119	0.95119
	0.95119	0.95119	0.95119	0.95119	0.95119	0.95119	0.95119	0.95119	0.95119
(1,1)	0.94619	0.94648	0.94648	0.94697	0.94745	0.94778	0.94738	0.94791	0.94881
	0.94590	0.94618	0.94647	0.94683	0.94722	0.94783	0.94735	0.94787	0.94877
	0.94553	0.94572	0.94606	0.94662	0.94695	0.94757	0.94731	0.94778	0.94854
(1,2)	0.85914	0.86147	0.86171	0.86266	0.86661	0.86860	0.86547	0.86956	0.87294
	0.85874	0.86069	0.86136	0.86279	0.86631	0.86798	0.86575	0.86970	0.87293
	0.85812	0.86022	0.86107	0.86227	0.86551	0.86718	0.86509	0.86876	0.87133
(2,0.5)	0.95105	0.95105	0.95105	0.95110	0.95115	0.95119	0.95110	0.95115	0.95119
	0.95110	0.95110	0.95110	0.95110	0.95115	0.95119	0.95110	0.95115	0.95119
	0.95105	0.95105	0.95105	0.95110	0.95115	0.95119	0.95110	0.95115	0.95119
(2,1)	0.93121	0.93292	0.93335	0.93360	0.93688	0.93845	0.93479	0.93827	0.94046
	0.93078	0.93282	0.93335	0.93321	0.93611	0.93769	0.93474	0.93821	0.94021
	0.92959	0.93150	0.93231	0.93268	0.93563	0.93706	0.93442	0.93761	0.93942
(2,2)	0.75871	0.76281	0.76323	0.76500	0.77104	0.77470	0.77044	0.77696	0.78314
	0.75743	0.76095	0.76191	0.76476	0.77075	0.77446	0.76974	0.77621	0.78211
	0.75658	0.76024	0.76229	0.76317	0.76859	0.77212	0.76955	0.77554	0.78063

All estimates are computed using 20,000 simulation runs. Bond prices are per face amount of one dollar. The upper value, middle value, and lower value in each cell are CAT bond prices computed when the interest rate elasticities of the asset are 0, –3, and –5, respectively.

measure the default risk premium by comparing with the values in the right-hand side panel of Table 2. Observe that the default risk premium decreases with the A/L ratio and increases with occurrence intensity and loss volatility. The default risk premium can go as high as 1,015 basis points for the case of A/L = 1.1, $(\lambda, \sigma_i) = (2,2)$, and $\phi = -5$.

TABLE 3

(Continued)

(λ,σ_i)	A/L = 1.1			A/L = 1.2			A/L = 1.3		
	Triggers								
	100	110	120	100	110	120	100	110	120
With Moral Hazard									
(0.5,0.5)	0.95119	0.95119	0.95119	0.95119	0.95119	0.95119	0.95119	0.95119	0.95119
	0.95119	0.95119	0.95119	0.95119	0.95119	0.95119	0.95119	0.95119	0.95119
	0.95119	0.95119	0.95119	0.95119	0.95119	0.95119	0.95119	0.95119	0.95119
(0.5,1)	0.94695	0.94738	0.94743	0.94746	0.94817	0.94841	0.94781	0.94853	0.94881
	0.94667	0.94705	0.94709	0.94726	0.94778	0.94792	0.94767	0.94838	0.94867
	0.94634	0.94672	0.94677	0.94712	0.94774	0.94788	0.94757	0.94824	0.94847
(0.5,2)	0.90139	0.90263	0.90273	0.90309	0.90518	0.90642	0.90432	0.90660	0.90822
	0.90118	0.90270	0.90284	0.90311	0.90511	0.90621	0.90458	0.90681	0.90838
	0.90058	0.90201	0.90244	0.90289	0.90484	0.90580	0.90411	0.90621	0.90754
(1,0.5)	0.95119	0.95119	0.95119	0.95119	0.95119	0.95119	0.95119	0.95119	0.95119
	0.95115	0.95115	0.95115	0.95115	0.95115	0.95115	0.95115	0.95115	0.95115
	0.95107	0.95107	0.95107	0.95115	0.95115	0.95115	0.95119	0.95119	0.95119
(1,1)	0.94004	0.94076	0.94095	0.94142	0.94251	0.94308	0.94236	0.94351	0.94489
	0.93988	0.94055	0.94074	0.94132	0.94232	0.94313	0.94222	0.94337	0.94456
	0.93955	0.94003	0.94050	0.94132	0.94222	0.94313	0.94214	0.94328	0.94442
(1,2)	0.84697	0.84892	0.84925	0.85073	0.85444	0.85615	0.85394	0.85770	0.85079
	0.84583	0.84759	0.84831	0.85054	0.85363	0.85525	0.85384	0.85750	0.86050
	0.84551	0.84727	0.84818	0.84988	0.85268	0.85426	0.85369	0.85698	0.85936
(2,0.5)	0.94988	0.95040	0.95040	0.95009	0.95080	0.95085	0.95010	0.95081	0.95091
	0.94390	0.94973	0.94973	0.94996	0.95058	0.95062	0.95010	0.95081	0.95091
	0.94900	0.94929	0.94934	0.94972	0.95039	0.95044	0.94999	0.95066	0.95075
(2,1)	0.90605	0.90928	0.90957	0.91001	0.91553	0.91767	0.91310	0.91891	0.92285
	0.90527	0.90875	0.90970	0.91020	0.91529	0.91743	0.91307	0.91877	0.92225
	0.90318	0.90599	0.90680	0.91002	0.91483	0.91735	0.91305	0.91861	0.92175
(2,2)	0.72243	0.72628	0.72690	0.72928	0.73584	0.74017	0.73542	0.74226	0.74883
	0.72064	0.72416	0.72521	0.72877	0.73463	0.73853	0.73456	0.74117	0.74702
	0.71921	0.72254	0.72440	0.72764	0.73278	0.73645	0.73378	0.74001	0.74539

To incorporate the effect of moral hazard, assume that when the accumulated loss amounts to 80 percent of the trigger level, the insurer will settle the catastrophe claims more generously and therefore will increase the expected loss of the catastrophe by 20 percent, i.e., $\alpha = 0.2$. The moral hazard therefore increases the default risk and lowers the bond price. For example, in the case of $(\lambda,\sigma_i) = (2,2)$, $\phi = -5$, the price decreases about 350 basis points with the moral hazard. The magnitude of the moral hazard effect increases with (λ, σ_i) and the absolute value of ϕ, and decreases with

FIGURE 1

Default-Risky CAT Bond Prices Without Moral Hazard $(\lambda, \sigma_i) = (2, 2), \Phi = -3$

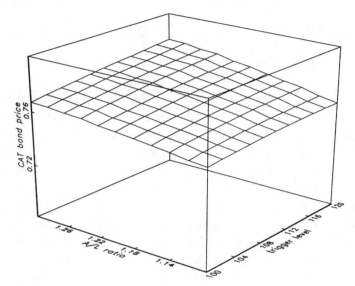

FIGURE 2

Default-Risky CAT Bond Prices With Moral Hazard $(\lambda, \sigma_i) = (2, 2), \Phi = -3$

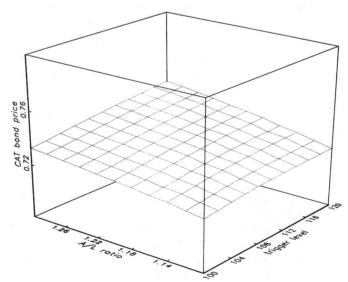

FIGURE 3

Default-Risky CAT Bond Prices With vs. Without Moral Hazard $(\lambda, \sigma_i) = (2, 2), \Phi = -3$

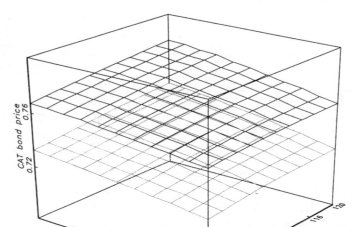

the A/L ratio. The CAT bond prices are illustrated, with and without moral hazard, under alternative parameter values in Figures 1 and 2, and both figures are combined into Figure 3 to show the price differences. The significant price differences indicate that the moral hazard is an important factor and should be taken into account when pricing the CAT bonds.[7]

Table 4 examines the impact of basis risks on CAT bond prices.[8] When the coefficient of correlation between the individual loss and the loss index ρ_x is low, the issuing firm has a high basis risk. When $\rho_x = 1$, no basis risk exists and the bond prices are supposed to be the same as their corresponding values in Table 3. In the case of $\rho_x = 0.8$ or 0.5, basis risk exits and we observe that it drives the CAT bond prices down and that its magnitude increases with the loss frequency and loss volatility. For example, in the case where $(\lambda, \sigma_i, \sigma_{index}) = (2,2,2)$, $K = 110$, and A/L $= 1.1$, the CAT bond price will drop 305 basis points when ρ_x decreases from 1 to 0.8 and fall another 170 basis points as 0.8 goes to 0.5. The price differences caused by the basis risk are substantial in this setting. Also observe that the effect of the basis risk decreases with the A/L ratios and increases with trigger levels, loss intensity, and loss volatility.

Figures 4, 5, and 6 show how the CAT bond prices relate to the basis risk (loss correlation, ρ_x) and the debt structure ratios (the amount of CAT bonds issued to the amount of total debt, a) for the case of $(\lambda, \sigma_i, \sigma_{index}) = (2,2,2)$ and $K = 110$. All three figures show that the CAT bond price increases with the loss correlation at an increasing rate. This indicates that the loss correlation decreases the basis risk premium at an increasing rate. It also implies that insurers with low loss correlation are subject to a substantial

---

[7] Bantwal and Kunreuther (1999) also pointed out that moral hazard may explain the CAT bond premium puzzle.

[8] Because the difference caused by the interest rate elasticity is small, the authors report only the case of $\phi = -3$ and focus the discussion on basis risks.

TABLE 4

Default-Risky CAT Bond Prices With Basis Risk ($\lambda_r = -0.01$, $\phi = -3$)

Trigger	100			110			120		
				ρ_x					
$(\lambda, \sigma_i, \sigma_{index})$	0.5	0.8	1	0.5	0.8	1	0.5	0.8	1
A/L = 1.1									
(0.5,0.5,0.5)	0.95122	0.95122	0.95122	0.95122	0.95122	0.95122	0.95122	0.95122	0.95122
(0.5,1,1)	0.94833	0.94854	0.94885	0.94853	0.94867	0.94906	0.94876	0.94873	0.94909
(0.5,2,2)	0.89340	0.89808	0.90726	0.89448	0.89859	0.90835	0.89582	0.90018	0.90881
(1,0.5,0.5)	0.95123	0.95123	0.95123	0.95123	0.95123	0.95123	0.95123	0.95123	0.95123
(1,1,1)	0.94327	0.94383	0.94552	0.94413	0.94467	0.94607	0.94458	0.94501	0.94622
(1,2,2)	0.83091	0.84144	0.85737	0.83322	0.84367	0.86005	0.83550	0.84510	0.86035
(2,0.5,0.5)	0.95127	0.95127	0.95127	0.95127	0.95127	0.95127	0.95127	0.95127	0.95127
(2,1,1)	0.92610	0.92876	0.93332	0.92861	0.93075	0.93523	0.93037	0.93200	0.93538
(2,2,2)	0.71399	0.73115	0.76071	0.71764	0.73464	0.76521	0.72309	0.73987	0.76738
A/L = 1.2									
(0.5,0.5,0.5)	0.95122	0.95122	0.95122	0.95122	0.95122	0.95122	0.95122	0.95122	0.95122
(0.5,1,1)	0.94865	0.94879	0.94904	0.94900	0.94910	0.94944	0.94934	0.94927	0.94965
(0.5,2,2)	0.89601	0.90057	0.90889	0.89748	0.90144	0.91058	0.89867	0.90283	0.91176
(1,0.5,0.5)	0.95123	0.95123	0.95123	0.95123	0.95123	0.95123	0.95123	0.95123	0.95123
(1,1,1)	0.94490	0.94530	0.94641	0.94571	0.94606	0.94711	0.94619	0.94655	0.94778
(1,2,2)	0.83695	0.84708	0.86075	0.83883	0.84902	0.86445	0.84213	0.85157	0.86749
(2,0.5,0.5)	0.95127	0.95127	0.95127	0.95127	0.95127	0.95127	0.95127	0.95127	0.95127
(2,1,1)	0.92922	0.93161	0.93491	0.93194	0.93388	0.93765	0.93394	0.93543	0.93883
(2,2,2)	0.72460	0.74141	0.76736	0.72943	0.74604	0.77496	0.73372	0.75033	0.77937
A/L = 1.3									
(0.5,0.5,0.5)	0.95122	0.95122	0.95122	0.95122	0.95122	0.95122	0.95122	0.95122	0.95122
(0.5,1,1)	0.94930	0.94939	0.94938	0.94963	0.94970	0.94973	0.94994	0.94984	0.94999
(0.5,2,2)	0.89902	0.90325	0.91039	0.90074	0.90456	0.91237	0.90157	0.90567	0.91386
(1,0.5,0.5)	0.95123	0.95123	0.95123	0.95123	0.95123	0.95123	0.95123	0.95123	0.95123
(1,1,1)	0.94552	0.94581	0.94663	0.94657	0.84683	0.94752	0.94693	0.94725	0.94835
(1,2,2)	0.84111	0.85106	0.86335	0.84427	0.85425	0.86782	0.84660	0.85582	0.87093
(2,0.5,0.5)	0.95127	0.95127	0.95127	0.95127	0.95127	0.95127	0.95127	0.95127	0.95127
(2,1,1)	0.93160	0.93371	0.93620	0.93448	0.93612	0.93898	0.93651	0.93776	0.94074
(2,2,2)	0.73357	0.74992	0.77300	0.73896	0.75536	0.78101	0.74393	0.76011	0.78757

All estimates are computed using 20,000 simulation runs. Bond prices are per face amount of one dollar.

discount in their CAT bond prices. These figures also show that the CAT bond price decreases with the debt structure ratio a at an increasing rate, especially at low A/L ratios (see Figure 4), indicating that CAT bond debt increases the default premium at

FIGURE 4

Default-Risky CAT Bond Prices With Basis Risk A/L = 1.1, K = 110, $\Phi = -3$, $(\lambda, \sigma_i, \sigma_{index}) = (2, 2, 2)$

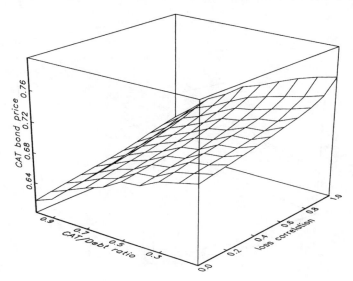

FIGURE 5

Default-Risky CAT Bond Prices With Basis Risk A/L = 1.2, K = 110, $\Phi = -3$, $(\lambda, \sigma_i, \sigma_{index}) = (2, 2, 2)$

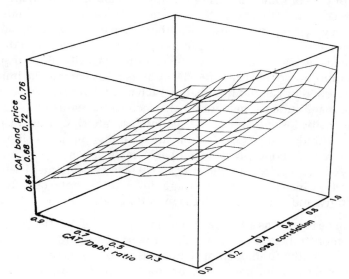

FIGURE 6

Default-Risky CAT Bond Prices With Basis Risk A/L = 1.3, K = 110, $\Phi = -3, (\lambda, \sigma_i, \sigma_{index}) = (2, 2, 2)$

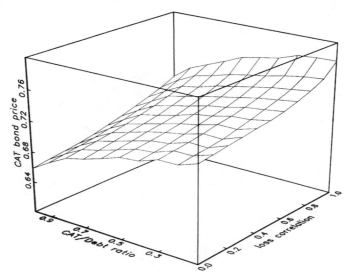

an increasing rate. Thus, insurers with more CAT bonds in debt need to pay a higher premium for their bonds.

CONCLUSION

This study develops a model to price CAT bonds under an environment of stochastic interest rates and more generic catastrophe loss processes. This model allows one to measure the impacts of default-risk, moral hazard, and basis risk that are associated with CAT bonds. The authors first compute the default-free CAT bond prices and find that the prices computed by using the approximating solution are very close to their numerical counterparts, except that when the loss volatility is high the approximating solution gives higher values. The authors then estimate the default-risky CAT bond prices and examine how the default risk premium changes with the catastrophe occurrence intensity, loss volatility, and interest rate elasticity of the insurer's assets, initial capital ratio, and debt structure. The authors also estimate the impact of moral hazard on CAT bond prices and find that moral hazard drives down bond prices substantially. The magnitude of this moral hazard effect increases with the catastrophe occurrence intensity, loss volatility, and the interest rate risk of the insurer's assets, and decreases with the trigger level and insurer's initial capital position. Finally, the authors compute CAT bond prices when basis risk is taken into account. The basis risk reduces CAT bond prices significantly and at a decreasing rate. The magnitude of the basis risk effect increases with the trigger level, catastrophe occurrence intensity, and loss volatility, and decreases with the initial capital position.

This model can be viewed as a general model in valuing default-risky debts; this study serves as a demonstration of its application. The structural framework in this model links bond prices to the fundamental characteristics of assets, liabilities, and interest rates and allows one to value bonds with unique features through the use of numerical analysis. The model can be easily extended to analyze other default-risky debts and insurance-linked securities.

References

American Academy of Actuaries, 1999, Bibliographic Report to the National Association of Insurance Commissioners—Insurance Securitization Working Group.

Bantwal, V. J., and H. C. Kunreuther, 1999, A CAT bond Premium Puzzle?, Working paper, Financial Institutions Center, The Wharton School, University of Pennsylvania.

Belonsky, G. M., 1998, Insurance-Linked Notes, *Journal of Insurance Regulation*, 17(2): 170-178.

Bouzouita, R., and A. J. Young, 1998, Catastrophe Insurance Options, *Journal of Insurance Regulation*, 16(3): 313-326.

Bowers, N. L., J. H. U. Gerber, J. C. Hickman, D. A. Jones, and C. J. Nesbitt, 1986, *Actuarial Mathematics* (Itasca, Ill.: Society of Actuaries).

Canter, M. S., J. B. Cole, and R. I. Sandor, 1997, Insurance Derivatives: A New Asset Class for the Capital Markets and a New Hedging Tool for the Insurance Industry, *Journal of Applied Corporate Finance*, 10: 69-83.

Chang, C., J. Chang, and M.-T. Yu, 1996, Pricing Catastrophe Insurance Futures Call Spreads: A Randomized Operational Time Approach, *Journal of Risk and Insurance*, 63(4): 599-617.

Cox, J., J. Ingersoll, and S. Ross, 1985, The Term Structure of Interest Rates, *Econometrica*, 53: 385-407.

Cox, J., and S. Ross, 1976, The Valuation of Options for Alternative Stochastic Processes, *Journal of Financial Economics*, 3: 145-166.

Cox, S. H., and H. W. Pedersen, 2000, Catastrophe Risk Bonds, *North American Actuarial Journal*, 4(4): 56-82.

Cox, S. H., and R. G. Schwebach, 1992, Insurance Futures and Hedging Insurance Price Risk, *Journal of Risk and Insurance*, 59: 628-644.

Cummins, J. D., 1988, Risk-Based Premiums for Insurance Guarantee Funds, *Journal of Finance*, 43: 593-607.

Cummins, J. D., and H. Geman, 1995, Pricing Catastrophe Futures and Call Spreads: An Arbitrage Approach, *Journal of Fixed Income*, 4: 46-57.

Davidson, R. J., 1998, Working Toward a Comprehensive National Strategy for Funding Catastrophe Exposures, *Journal of Insurance Regulation*, 17(2): 134-170.

Doherty, N. A., 1997, Financial Innovation in the Management of Catastrophe Risk, *Journal of Applied Corporate Finance*, 10: 84-95.

Duan, J. C., A. Moreau, and C. W. Sealey, 1995, Deposit Insurance and Bank Interest Rate Risk: Pricing and Regulatory Implication, *Journal of Banking and Finance*, 19: 1091-1108.

Harrison, J. M., and S. R. Pliska, 1981, Martingales and Stochastic Integrals in the Theory of Continuous Trading, *Stochastic Processes and Their Applications*, 11: 215-260.

Jarrow, R., and A. Rudd, 1982, Approximate Option Valuation for Arbitrary Stochastic Processes, *Journal of Financial Economics*, 10: 347-369.

Laurenzano, V. L., 1998, Securitization of Insurance Risk: A Perspective for Regulator, *Journal of Insurance Regulation*, 17(2): 179-185.

Litzenberger, R. H., D. R. Beaglehole, and C. E. Reynolds, 1996, Assessing Catastrophe Reinsurance-Linked Securities as a New Asset Class, *Journal of Portfolio Management*, 23(3): 76-86.

Loubergé, H., E. Kellezi, and M. Gilli, 1999, Using Catastrophe-Linked Securities to Diversify Insurance Risk: A Financial Analysis of CAT bonds, *Journal of Insurance Issues* 22(2): 125-146.

Merton, R., 1976, Option Pricing When Underlying Stock Returns Are Discontinuous, *Journal of Financial Economics*, 3: 125-144.

Merton, R., 1977, An Analytic Derivation of the Cost of Deposit Insurance and Loan Guarantee, *Journal of Banking and Finance*, 1: 3-11.

Naik, V., and M. Lee, 1990, General Equilibrium Pricing of Options on the Market Portfolio With Discontinuous Returns, *Review of Financial Studies*, 3(4): 493-521.

Nielson, J., and K. Sandmann, 1996, The Pricing of Asian Options Under Stochastic Interest Rate, *Applied Mathematical Finance*, 3: 209-236.

Ritchken, P., 1996, *Derivative Markets: Theory, Strategy, and Applications* (New York: Harper Collins).

Turnbull, S., and L. Wakeman, 1991, A Quick Algorithm for Pricing European Average Options, *Journal of Financial and Quantitative Analysis*, 26: 377-389.

Vasicek, O. A., 1977, An Equilibrium Characterization of Term Structure, *Journal of Financial Economics*, 5: 177-188.

Zajdenweber, D., 1998, The Valuation of Catastrophe-Reinsurance-Linked Securities, Paper presented at American Risk and Insurance Association Meeting.

©The Journal of Risk and Insurance, 2002, Vol. 69, No. 1, 45-62

Insurance Contracts and Securitization

Neil A. Doherty
Harris Schlesinger

Abstract

High correlations between risks can increase required insurer capital and/or reduce the availability of insurance. For such insurance lines, securitization is rapidly emerging as an alternative form of risk transfer. The ultimate success of securitization in replacing or complementing traditional insurance and reinsurance products depends on the ability of securitization to facilitate and/or be facilitated by insurance contracts. The authors consider how insured losses might be decomposed into separate components, one of which is a type of "systemic risk" that is highly correlated among insureds. Such a correlated component might conceivably be hedged directly by individuals but is more likely to be hedged by the insurer. The authors examine how insurance contracts may be designed to allow the insured a mechanism to retain all or part of the systemic component. Examples are provided that illustrate this methodology in several types of insurance markets subject to systemic risk.

Introduction

Insurance markets are undergoing a transformation as new risk management strategies are formulated and new financial instruments are created to supplement and/or replace traditional insurance/reinsurance products. This article takes a normative look at these emerging strategies and markets. In particular, the authors explain how an unbundling of the aggregate insured risk leads to a greater ability to lay off the unwanted parts of the risk. While this type of risk decomposition and risk management is becoming more fashionable to insurers, the authors show how an innovation in current insurance contracting can help facilitate improved risk retention on the part of insureds. In many cases, this innovation leads to results that mimic full access to financial risk management markets directly by the insureds.

An important driver of this innovation is an impaired ability of traditional insurance markets to cope with highly correlated risks. For example, reevaluations of catastrophe

Neil Doherty and Harris Schlesinger work at the University of Pennsylvania and the University of Alabama, respectively. The authors thank seminar participants at the Universities of Konstanz, Munich, and Toulouse as well as at Tulane University for helpful comments on an earlier version of this article. Comments from Henri Loubergé and from three anonymous reviewers were especially helpful.

exposures following events such as Hurricane Andrew and the Northridge earthquake suggest the plausibility of single catastrophes on the order of $50–100 billion. Yet the total net worth of the entire property-liability insurance industry is only on the order of $300 billion. While such losses are large enough to overwhelm the insurance industry, the appeal of securitizing this risk becomes apparent when one considers that losses of this magnitude are less than one standard deviation of the daily value traded in U.S. capital markets.[1]

A similar demand for insurance substitutes arises in the market for general liability insurance. An implicit correlation arises from the changes in liability rules against which new claims will be resolved through new precedents and/or new legislation. Such rule changes have a common effect on whole groups of policyholders. For example, a legal precedent that extends common-law liability rules will apply to all subsequent suits in the same jurisdiction, unless overruled by a higher court. This judicial instability=lies at the heart of the periodic availability crises that have been experienced in liability insurance markets. Yet in today's marketplace, insurers are currently expanding their liability insurance offerings to ever broader classes of insureds, especially in the area of professional liability. Moreover, these lines of insurance are becoming more specialized, such as in liability products for financial services, technology, and telecommunications (see Hofmann, 1996). Obviously, this specialization is partly a function of marketing strategy, but the results in this article imply that such specialization could also be an attempt to take advantage of the stronger correlations present within a more narrowly defined risk class. These narrower risk classes lend themselves more readily to the formation of new securitized products, based on an index of the correlated risk. The high correlation of the individual risk with the index mitigates the problem of basis risk.[2]

Another example of correlation occurs in the area of property insurance at replacement cost. Unanticipated changes in prices, as well as changes in fixed costs such as permit fees for rebuilding damaged real property, will likely affect all indemnity costs. Again, such changes in prices and costs are common to a group of insureds. Even if the absolute level of correlation for certain types of losses is relatively low, it may be fairly easy to factor out these highly correlated components of the losses and thus design products that improve insurer efficiency. An analogous situation exists in the market for health insurance.

Each case above has a systemic component of the collection of risks being pooled. When correlation exists between loss exposures, the optimal type of risk-sharing contract is one in which the risk can be decomposed into diversifiable and nondiversifiable parts, with the former fully insured and the latter shared with the insurer. This is the essence of mutual insurance.[3] One can think of this sharing arrangement as one in which all individuals fully insure their idiosyncratic risk but receive a dividend from their insurer that is scaled to the aggregate experience of the insurance pool. Such

---

[1] See, for example, Cummins, Doherty, and Lo (2001) and Froot (2001).

[2] Basis risk need not be all bad. It may, for example, help to alleviate moral hazard problems. However, such issues go beyond the scope of this article. See Doherty (1997) for further discussion.

[3] See, for example, Borch (1962), Marshall (1974), Smith and Stultzer (1990), and Dionne and Doherty (1993).

contracts are called *participating policies* and are fairly common for many types of insurance. The innovation in this article is that the authors allow for an endogenous level of participation, whereby the insured can choose a convex mixture of a fixed-premium contract and a participating policy. This *variable participation contract* allows the individual to selectively hedge both the diversifiable and nondiversifiable risk components.

The process of securitization entails the decomposition and repackaging of risk. Securitization can entail both the direct packaging of an individual insurer's loss liabilities for sale in the capital market or designing securitized products based on some economic index. Obviously, securitization is often a substitute for reinsurance in that it allows for insurers to transfer excess risk. However, securitization can offer an ability to carve out pieces of the risk, rather than treating the risk as a whole. In particular, the authors show how this ability to carve out the risk allows for an increase in consumer welfare.

Since securitization relies on the decomposition of risks, a knowledge of the mathematical structure of the loss correlations becomes important. Different mathematical structures may require different markets and different contracts to achieve efficient risk sharing. If losses can be decomposed into two additive components, one independent among insureds and the other highly correlated, then variable participation contracts can be replicated through the combination of a traditional nonparticipating insurance policy and a futures contract to hedge the systemic risk component. In this case, policyholders can, at least in theory, assemble the optimal hedge on their own account.[4] If the two risk components are multiplicative, replicating the variable participation contract on the individual's own account may still be possible, but this will require insurer intermediation. As this article explains, efficient securitization requires that any systemic risk first be pooled through insurance. The optimal package is then a variable participation contract for the insured together with a futures contract for the insurer covering the aggregate policyholders' dividend risk. Thus, securitization will likely involve the sale of insurance derivatives to primary insurers, and these instruments will compete with, or complement, traditional reinsurance products. Given the relative size of capital markets as compared with that of reinsurance markets, securitization is clearly a necessary component. Indeed, reinsurers will also likely benefit by turning to capital markets themselves.

The focus herein is on how insurance contracts can be redesigned to improve efficiency. Although the authors do not consider the effects of this improved design on supply and demand within the insurance market *per se*, insurance companies that do not keep up with design improvements clearly stand to lose market share. Although the authors examine the effects of securitization in markets for which the systemic part of the decomposed risk (be it additive or multiplicative) is perfectly correlated, the

---

[4] Although securitization may also affect markets through reductions in transaction costs (including agency costs), as compared to traditional insurance products, this is not a focus of the current article. Instead, the authors focus on the value of securitization aside from any effects upon transaction costs. Since transaction costs associated with insurance have often run on the order of 30 percent of premiums, the authors do not mean to imply that securitized products cannot have a large effect on cost efficiency. See, for example, Niehaus and Mann (1992) and Froot (2001).

authors also show how imperfect correlations introduce a type of basis risk. The authors conclude by considering several commonly known real-world examples of insurance markets that exhibit correlation, and the authors conjecture how the empirical pattern of securitization might develop.

ADDITIVE SYSTEMIC RISK

This theoretical analysis of optimal hedging uses only the assumptions of risk aversion, defined as an aversion to mean-preserving spreads, and of a preference for higher levels of wealth. In other words, consumers have a preference for second-degree stochastic dominance. The authors allow for risk aversion of both order 1 and order 2, as defined by Segal and Spivak (1990), which has the advantage of allowing for very generalized results. Results within particular frameworks, such as expected-utility theory, smooth nonlinear preference functionals (Machina, 1982), rank-dependent expected utility (Quiggin, 1982), and the dual theory (Yaari, 1987), are all obtainable as special cases.[5]

The securitization of insurance risk is at issue when risk can be decomposed into an idiosyncratic component and a systemic element that can be indexed. The authors consider two forms of this decomposition: additive and multiplicative. These forms carry different implications for the design of insurance derivatives, and they are useful in accessing well-known results on optimal hedging behavior. In this section, the authors consider the case in which the risk decomposition is additive. The authors examine the multiplicative case in the following section.

Let (Ω, F, μ) be a probability space, and consider the measurable functions $L: \Omega \to [t, T]$ and $\varepsilon: \Omega \to [-s, s]$, $t, T, s \in \mathcal{R}$. Let L and ε denote the random variables so defined. Consider an individual with initial wealth $W > 0$ that is subject to a loss of size $L + \varepsilon$; assume here that the scalars t, T, and s are chosen such that $0 \le t - s \le T + s \le W$.[6]

An infinitely large population of consumers with identical loss distributions exists. Refer to this population as the risk pool, and assume that the idiosyncratic random loss components L_i are mutually independent from one another, so that L_i for the ith individual is independent from that of the jth individual, L_j. However, the second components of the loss decomposition are equal for all individuals, i.e., perfectly positively correlated, $\varepsilon_i = \varepsilon_j$. Assume that $E(\varepsilon) = 0$, where E denotes the expectation operator, and that ε and L are independent of one another for all individuals. Since ε is identical for all individuals, suppress its subscript. For example, if $\varepsilon = 100$, then losses are 100 higher for everyone. Although this additive case is less realistic than the multiplicative case that follows, it will be useful for establishing later results.

The authors will consider various scenarios for interpreting ε. A word of caution is in order here. The case in which $\varepsilon = 0$ need not be "expected" in any sense except as a long-run average. Indeed, the distribution of ε may be highly skewed. For example, in modeling catastrophes, one might think of ε as being slightly negative in almost every

---

[5] See Machina (1995), Karni (1995), and Schlesinger (1997) for summaries of insurance results in these models.

[6] The authors make this last assumption to avoid complications of modeling limited liability. The authors also wish to discourage thinking of ε as a loss amount itself. It is simply an adjustment to the long-run average loss that is experienced within a given year.

year. It might then be positive and large only on rare occasions. Hence, $\varepsilon = 0$ in no way should be interpreted as a "typical year," or as a "forecast" for the year. One can view the catastrophe example as follows: Over the years, the average loss per individual insured is $E(L + \varepsilon) = EL$. However, the average loss is not stable over time, so that in many years it is less than EL, whereas in some years, and most notably catastrophe years, the average annual loss exceeds EL. For cases in which ε may represent an unexpected change in price levels, it may be more natural to assume that ε is slightly positive or negative with equal probability. Thus, this modeling of the "ε risk" is meant to be rather general.

Optimal Risk Sharing With Consumer Access to Securitization

Suppose first that separate markets exist for hedging the risks L and ε. Assuming competitive markets, postulate an insurance market for L with actuarially fair pricing. In such a market, full insurance is purchased on L. This holds regardless of the treatment used for ε and regardless of whether risk aversion is of first or second order.[7] To hedge the systemic risk component ε, postulate the existence of a futures market. Assuming a clientele of only speculators and individuals endowed with ε risk, such a futures market will exhibit normal backwardation, due to the natural hedging demand by insureds. Model this backwardation as replacing the random loss component ε with a fixed certain loss of $\gamma > 0$.[8] What the authors envision here is a world in which the ε risk might not be fully diversifiable in global markets but can be reduced enough to allow insurability of the ε component. Cummins and Weiss (2000) label these two cases as "globally diversifiable" and "globally insurable," respectively. Froot (2001) examines several reasons why γ might be lower in the capital markets as opposed to in traditional reinsurance markets.

Futures contracts are assumed to be fully divisible, and individuals choose the fraction of systemic risk ε that they wish to hedge on their own account. Because this article is using a static model and assuming perfect correlation of the ε risk, assume away problems associated with basis risk due to the timing of futures contracts or to the imperfect nature of the hedge instrument. Final wealth Y is thus given as

$$Y = W - EL - [b\gamma + (1 - b)\varepsilon], \tag{1}$$

where b denotes the fraction of ε hedged in the futures market, i.e., the hedge ratio. Since $\gamma > 0$ and $E(\varepsilon) = 0$, if preferences satisfy second-order risk aversion, then the

---

[7] Doherty and Schlesinger (1983) prove this result for a model using differentiable expected utility. Since full coverage for any treatment of ε is optimal for all risk averters defined via expected utility, it follows from Zilcha and Chew (1990, Theorem 1) that such behavior is optimal for the broader class of risk-averse preferences examined here. The result still holds if the utility function is not differentiable everywhere, which follows from Segal and Spivak (1990).

[8] If many pools of insureds exist, each with an ε that is independent of other groups', then γ possibly equals zero. The authors assume that a larger market does not exist to "pass off" the ε risk, so that $\gamma > 0$. The authors also do not consider a general equilibrium model, in which the existence of the types of contracts proposed in this article have an effect on market prices, including a type of feedback effect upon γ itself.

optimal hedge ratio equals $b^* < 1$. If risk aversion is of order 1, then $b^* < 1$, with the possibility of complete hedging, $b^* = 1$.[9]

Variable Participation Contracts

Since real-world futures markets are not likely to exist for hedging only a part of an individual's loss, the article examines an alternative contract available through the insurance market. In particular, the individual may buy insurance via a participating insurance contract. The innovation that is presented here is to make the degree of participation a choice variable of the individual. To this end, assume that insurers are willing to offer insurance with zero participation, with a market-determined premium loading factor of $\lambda > 0$. Since the total individual loss is $L + \varepsilon$ with ε identical (i.e., perfectly correlated) for all individuals, the market charges the risk premium λ for this ε component of the total loss. Assume here that, although the reinsurance market and capital market can absorb the ε risk, it cannot be fully diversified away. Since the L are all independent and identically distributed (i.i.d.), there is no additional amount of premium loading required due to the L; rather, the L risks are fully diversifiable due to the assumed infinite number of independent risks. For simplicity, no other transaction costs exist in this model.

Consider now a fully participating policy with a premium equal to the *ex post* average indemnity paid by the insurer. Such a premium is (essentially) $\alpha(EL + \varepsilon)$, where the EL term is (essentially) guaranteed by the law of large numbers.[10] Since the individual bears all of the ε risk in this case, the competitive-market insurance premium loading is zero. Rather than imposing zero or full participation, allow the individual to choose the degree of participation in the insurance market by setting the total premium P as follows:

$$P = \alpha[\beta(1 + \lambda)EL + (1 - \beta)(EL + \varepsilon)] = \alpha\{EL + [\beta\lambda EL + (1 - \beta)\varepsilon]\}, \tag{2}$$

where α denotes the proportion of loss indemnified by the insurer and where $\beta \in [0,1]$ is a choice variable of the individual denoting the degree of participation, with $\beta = 1$ denoting a fixed premium and $\beta = 0$ noting full participation. The insurance policy

---

[9] These conclusions follow easily along the lines suggested in note 7. Note that in Equation (1) only one source of uncertainty exists—ε. Note also that risk aversion is of order 1 if

$$\lim_{t \to 0^+} \pi'(tx) = 0,$$

where the limit is taken over positive values of t, x is a zero-mean random variable, $\pi(tx)$ is the risk premium such that $-\pi(tx) \sim tx$, and $\pi'(tx)$ denotes $\partial\pi(tx)/\partial t$ for $t > 0$. Risk aversion is of order 2 if $\pi'(0x) = 0$ but $\pi''(0x) \neq 0$. See Segal and Spivak (1990).

[10] More realistically, one would need to be concerned with the timing of premium collections and indemnity payouts. However, the authors abstract from these nuances in the static model. The total premium as given above is random *ex ante*. The premium actually paid *ex post* is dependent on the realized value of ε. One can think of the individual paying an up-front premium of αEL. The individual is then assessed an extra premium of $\alpha\varepsilon$. In the case where $\varepsilon < 0$, this "assessment" is paid to the individual as a dividend. A negative modal value of ε would thus correspond to the payment of a dividend in most years under participating policies.

with a premium defined by Equation (2) is called a *variable participation contract*.[11] Final wealth Y is given by

$$Y = W - P - (1 - \alpha)(L + \varepsilon) = [W - \alpha EL - (1 - \alpha)L] - \varepsilon + \alpha\beta(\varepsilon - \lambda EL). \qquad (3)$$

It is interesting to note in the decomposition in Equation (3) that, although the fixed insurance premium depends upon the loading factor λ, the λ only attaches itself to the ε risk in the decomposition. In other words, it is "as if" the individual is being offered fair insurance against the L risk, with a price for eliminating ε risk. This point is revisited in Equation (4) below.

Suppose that $\alpha \neq 0$, and suppose for the moment that one does not require $\beta \in [0,1]$. Then note that the value of α in the last term in Equation (3) is irrelevant, since it can be "undone" by a choice of β. In particular, letting $\delta = \alpha\beta$, the choice variables in Equation (3) are effectively α and δ, so long as $\alpha \neq 0$.

For any fixed value of δ, the terms $-\varepsilon + \delta(\varepsilon - \lambda EL)$ are a random background risk, whereas the first three terms on the right-hand side of Equation (3), in brackets, represent the standard insurance choice problem with an actuarial fair premium. Thus, for any fixed value of δ, the optimal insurance level is $\alpha^* = 1$, i.e., full coverage.[12]

Now since $\alpha^* = 1$, the assumption of $\alpha \neq 0$ is redundant and the relaxation of the condition $\beta \in [0,1]$ is irrelevant: The optimal β equals the optimal value of δ. Indeed, write Equation (3), under the assumption of full insurance coverage for any value of δ (i.e., any value of β), as

$$Y = W - EL - [\beta\lambda EL + (1 - \beta)\varepsilon]. \qquad (4)$$

Compare Equation (4) with Equation (1) and assume that the market risk premium for ε risk would be the same, whether in a futures market or in an insurance market; i.e., assume that $\lambda EL = \gamma$. By using a variable participation contract, the mutual insurance market provides the exact same set of alternatives and same optimal solution (with $\alpha^* = 1$ and $\beta^* = b^*$) as obtains in two separate markets. Of course, if $\lambda EL \neq \gamma$, then the cheaper alternative is likely to be the one that prevails in the marketplace.

One might approximate the variable participation strategy by buying a fixed-premium contract and simply buying shares of the insurer's stock, if it is a stock insurance company. However, stock prices include a broader view of company profitability and, in particular, a longer-term perspective. Thus, this strategy is likely to be dominated by one that develops a participation measure based on only the current aggregate L and ε development.

Market Structure With Additive Risk

The optimal variable participation contract entails full coverage, $\alpha^* = 1$, and $\beta = \beta^*$, which implies that some portion, β^*, of the systemic risk is transferred to external

---

[11] Of course, the individual may be able to self-construct an equivalent contract via the purchase of two separate contracts, one fixed-premium contract with coverage level $\beta\alpha$ and one fully participating contract with coverage level $1 - \beta\alpha$.

[12] This follows as in note 7.

investors. Two common mechanisms within the insurance industry are available for achieving this division of systemic risk. First, the insurer can be a stock insurer that issues a variable participation policy with portions $1 - \beta^*$ and β^* of the systemic risk allocated respectively to policyholders and to shareholders. Second, the insurer can be a mutual company that reinsures a portion β^* of its portfolio risk with independent stock reinsurers, thus passing the hedged systemic risk to the reinsurer's shareholders. Using securitization to handle the systemic risk would not affect the fundamental division of risk between policyholders and external investors (absent changes in transaction costs). Rather, securitization would achieve this division through a different set of contractual arrangements.

Although replication of the variable participation contract in separate markets also requires some insurance, securitization of the ε risk can be handled independently from the insurance contract. Whether the optimal contract is achieved via nonparticipating insurance with insureds hedging the ε risk directly in the futures market or via variable participation contracts with insurer-based securitization is likely to depend upon which method is more cost-effective once transaction costs are introduced. At least preliminary casual empirical evidence seems to support the latter. Moreover, a policy paying an indemnity based on L alone, rather than on $L + \varepsilon$, cannot adjust its claims until ε is learned *ex post*. Although $L + \varepsilon$ is observed immediately following a loss, one does not know the decomposition into L and ε until the end of the year, when the insurer has the data to observe $EL + \varepsilon$ for the year. A consumer is likely to prefer a current indemnity payment for the observed loss of $L + \varepsilon$, as presently exists, followed by an adjustment for ε (via a dividend or an assessment) at a later date. In theory, participation may require the insured to make additional large payments (assessments) after the policy period has expired, which are generally unacceptable to insurance regulators. More commonly, an insurer may "build in" most of the possible assessment as part of the insurance premium. This amount is then later refunded as a policy dividend (see note 9).

MULTIPLICATIVE SYSTEMIC RISK

Now assume that the insurable loss is of the form $(1 + \varepsilon)L$, where $E\varepsilon = 0$ and ε is independent of L_i for all i; L_i are independent and identically distributed, and ε is identical (perfectly correlated) across all insureds.[13] Thus, for example, if $\varepsilon = 0.05$, then everyone's realized loss is 5 percent higher than the long-run average. Final wealth Y in this case is given as

$$Y = W - (1 + \varepsilon)L = W - L - \varepsilon L. \tag{5}$$

Variable Participation Contracts

Maintaining the notation where $\beta = 1$ denotes a fixed premium and $\beta = 0$ denotes a fully participating policy, write the premium for coverage level α as

$$P = \alpha[\beta(1 + \lambda)EL + (1 - \beta)(EL)(1 + \varepsilon)] = \alpha EL\{1 + [\beta\lambda + (1 - \beta)\varepsilon]\}. \tag{6}$$

---

[13] A sketch of the model in this section appears in Schlesinger (1999), who used it to examine losses from natural catastrophes.

Thus the consumer's wealth after the purchase of insurance is

$$Y = W - \alpha EL - (1 - \alpha)(1 + \varepsilon)L - \alpha EL[\beta\lambda + (1 - \beta)\varepsilon] \tag{7}$$

or equivalently

$$Y = (1 + \varepsilon)[W - \alpha EL - (1 - \alpha)L)] - \varepsilon W - \alpha\beta EL[\lambda - \varepsilon]. \tag{8}$$

As in the previous section, suppose for now that $\alpha \neq 0$. Then note that the value of α in the last term in Equation (8) is irrelevant, since it can be "undone" by a choice of β. Once again letting $\delta = \alpha\beta$, the choice variables in Equation (8) are effectively α and δ, so long as $\alpha \neq 0$.

For any fixed value of δ, the last two terms in Equation (8) are a background risk, although the mean of this background risk is not zero. Note also that this background risk is linear in ε. The first term in Equation (8) has the same expected value for all choices of α. Let $H(\alpha)$ denote the random variable $W\alpha EL - (1 - \alpha)L$, and let $F(\varepsilon)$ denote the last two terms in Equation (8). Thus Equation (8) can be written as $(1 + \varepsilon)H(\alpha) + F(\varepsilon)$. Because ε is statistically independent of L, it is statistically independent of H as well. Since $H(\alpha)$ has the same mean for all α, it follows from standard stochastic-dominance arguments that choosing $\alpha = 1$ will second-order-dominate every other choice of α for final wealth.[14] Consequently, $\alpha^* = 1$ is optimal for any risk averter for a fixed level of δ. Now, since $\alpha^* = 1$, the assumption here that $\alpha \neq 0$ is redundant. From Equation (7), using $\alpha^* = 1$, $\delta^* = \beta^* < 1$, with $\beta^* = 1$ only in the case where preferences satisfy first-order risk aversion.

Optimal Risk Sharing With Consumer Access to Securitization

First establish that the individual cannot replicate the variable participation contract simply by purchase of a nonparticipating policy and a separate futures contract on ε. Since the individual's wealth prospect is $W - L - \varepsilon L$, a simple policy fully covering $L\varepsilon$ (i.e., replacing L with EL) must be supplemented with a futures hedge written not simply on ε but on $L\varepsilon$. In other words, the task facing the individual is to hedge a random number of units of the ε risk. One is left with a random optimal hedge ratio; i.e., the hedge ratio β ideally would need to be scaled according to the idiosyncratic and random L. In theory, financial markets could write contracts based jointly on the realizations of ε and L, but this would involve monitoring each individual's losses by the financial market, which is likely to be inefficient. However, it is possible for the insurer, who already tracks individual loss data, to intermediate here.

A market could relatively easily emerge in which contracts written on the ε risk are traded between individual investors and insurance companies, with the insurers also offering participating contracts. Note that each individual has a stochastically identical multiplicative term $L_i\varepsilon$, and that the L_i are all independent from one another and

---

[14] Since all choices of α leave the mean of $H(\alpha)$ and thus of Y in Equation (8) unchanged, second-order stochastic dominance follows from Rothschild and Stiglitz (1970, Theorem 2), since one can write

$$(1 + \varepsilon)H(\alpha) + F(\varepsilon) = (1 + \varepsilon)H(1) + F(\varepsilon) + [H(\alpha) - H(1)](1 + \varepsilon),$$

where $E\{[(H(\alpha) - H(1))(1 + \varepsilon)] \mid (1 + \varepsilon)H(1) + F(\varepsilon)\} = E\{[(H(\alpha) - H(1))(1 + \varepsilon)] \mid \varepsilon\} = 0 \,\forall\varepsilon.$

from ε. It follows that there should be no risk-bearing cost in a competitive market (absent any transaction costs) for pooling the L risk.[15] To see this, define $£ \equiv \sum L_i / n$ and note that $E(£) = EL_i$. Now $VAR(£) = (VARL_i)/n \to 0$ as $n \to \infty$, since the L_i are independent and identically distributed. It follows that, in the limit,

$$VAR(£ + \varepsilon£) = (EL)^2 VAR(\varepsilon).$$

Thus, for the insurer, $£$ can be approximated as a constant, and one can write $£ + \varepsilon£$ in the approximate form $E(L) + \varepsilon E(L)$. In other words, each individual could pool his or her own εL_i and assume $\varepsilon E(L)$. That is, the individual swaps a random level of ε risk for a fixed level of ε risk. A competitive insurance market, in which participating policies are traded, could organize such pooling, for example. Under a pure mutual, with all idiosyncratic risk insured ($\alpha = 1$) and all systemic risk assumed by policyholders as dividends ($\beta = 0$), the individual's wealth would be

$$Y = W - EL - \varepsilon WL. \tag{9}$$

Letting ε' denote εEL and noting that ε' satisfies all of the requisite properties of ε for the case of additive risk components, it follows that the multiplicative risk component case is identical to the additive case, with ε' replacing ε. Thus, assuming a competitive insurance market and a futures market for ε that exhibits normal backwardation, the individual buys full insurance, $\alpha^* = 1$, together with an optimal futures market hedge, b^*, the optimal hedge ratio b for Equation (1), where here $\gamma = \lambda EL$ and $\varepsilon' = \varepsilon EL$ replaces ε. In other words, Equation (1) becomes

$$Y = W - EL - EL[b\lambda + (1 - b)\varepsilon]. \tag{10}$$

Note that Equation (10) is equivalent to Equation (7), with $\alpha^* = 1$. Thus, $b^* = \beta^*$ and once again the result is that two markets are equivalent to one insurance market with variable participating contracts. However, now the individual cannot readily access the futures market without help from the insurer (or some other financial intermediary) in pooling the random amount of ε risk, $L_i \varepsilon$.

Market Structure With Multiplicative Risk

To achieve the optimal contract ($\alpha^* = 1$, $\beta^* = b^*$) requires that the systemic risk of insureds be pooled, $\varepsilon' = \varepsilon EL$. This leads to two potential optimal contracting patterns. First, individuals can form a pure mutual insurance company, in which all systemic risk is passed back to policyholders in the form of dividends. Thus, each policyholder's wealth is $Y = W - EL - \varepsilon EL$, with the last term, εEL, being the dividend risk. Policyholders can then hedge a portion b^* of the dividend risk by trading on their own individual accounts. Second, the insurer can issue participating policies and can purchase a futures contract in the ratio β^* and pass the unhedged portion of the systemic risk $(1 - \beta^*)$ back to the policyholder in the form of a dividend. With either structure, the individual's wealth prospect is as shown in Equation (10). However, the essential

---

[15] Of course, as n gets larger, so does the variance of total losses. This would lead to a higher bankruptcy risk absent any increase in insurer capital. Assume $n \to \infty$ to circumvent this issue.

features of both contract structures are that the optimal contract can be assembled only if the systemic risk is pooled and insurers issue participating policies. Insurer intermediation is thus an essential component in securitizing the ε risk.

SECURITIZATION IN INSURANCE MARKETS: SOME EXAMPLES

Securitization is relatively new, and its full impact upon the business of insurance has yet to be fully determined. The authors believe current uses of securitization are still in the formative stages and have not yet fully self-developed within the marketplace. In this section, the three examples of insurance markets with correlated risks that were mentioned in the introduction are considered: (i) property insurance at replacement cost, (ii) liability insurance, and (iii) insurance for natural catastrophes. To the best of the authors' knowledge, only (iii) has been examined much at all in the literature. Each example is modeled using "multiplicative risk components." In each case, the authors examine how securitization and insurance contracting might work in an optimal setting.

Property Insurance at Replacement Cost

A futures market for any ε risk requires that it be clearly indexed. A very simple case is that in which policyholders are exposed to independent and identically distributed losses when measured in constant dollars, but in which a random (unexpected) inflation rate impacts all claims. The impact of inflation on each policyholder will depend on the size of each loss. This is clearly a case in which the systemic risk and the non-systemic risk are multiplicatively related. A random draw is taken from the inflation index, ε, and each constant dollar loss, L_i, is multiplied by the same revealed $(1 + \varepsilon)$. For example, if the realized value of ε is 0.05, then all loss claims cost 5 percent more than expected.

One way for insurers to handle the ε risk is to issue replacement-cost policies and to hedge the inflation risk themselves through options and/or futures markets. However, this approach may be costly to the insureds, who would prefer bearing some of the inflation risk themselves. At the other extreme, the policyholder could purchase an insurance contract that offered indemnification in constant dollars, such as one with an *ex ante* listing of insured values (a so-called valued policy, in the insurance world). However, the individual then would not have a fixed amount of ε risk to hedge in the futures market. If the insurer issues a participating replacement-cost policy, and insureds choose their own level of participation, $1 - \beta^*$, the insurer then can hedge the remaining portion β^* of the ε risk with some type of inflation-index derivative. Since the amounts of ε risk assumed by the insurer on individual policies are independent and are identically distributed except for a scaling factor due to differences in individual β_i, the insurer has (essentially) a fixed amount of ε risk to hedge.

Of course, in reality any type of inflation index will not affect all insured losses in the exactly same manner (i.e., the ε_i correlations will not be perfect), so that derivative securities on such an index will not be a perfect hedge. In the case of futures markets, the hedging strategy faces an added *basis risk*. Although such basis risk cannot be eliminated, it is possible that more restricted indexes will induce a more perfect correlation. For example, an inflation index on automobile parts would be a more efficient hedging instrument for automobile collision coverages than would a general consumer price index (CPI). Given their potential hedging purposes, one might therefore expect to see derivative products arise that are based on more specialized price indexes. Unfortunately, options and futures written directly on price index have not yet seemed to have taken hold in real-world markets. A highly touted futures contract on the CPI, introduced in 1985, quickly failed, due to a lack of trading volume. However, other recent products, such as the U.S. Treasury's issue of inflation-indexed government bonds, may either prove to be viable hedging instruments on their own or at least increase the potential demand for inflation-index derivatives to the point where such derivatives are commercially viable.

Liability Insurance

The case of implicit correlation caused by changes in liability rules is more complex. Obviously, changes in liability rules can affect both the likelihood of verdicts and the average size of jury awards. Only the latter effect is considered here, although it is recognized that the former effect is likely to be just as important.[16] Imagine that an index is taken of the changes in average liability awards (IALA), which corresponds to ε. If one assumes that the events that give rise to liability awards are stable (so that the number of awards is unaffected), one can discount individual awards by the IALA index to derive a "stable liability regime" (SLR) award. Accordingly, the SLR claims, i.e., the L_i, will be independent and identically distributed (or, more realistically, at least independent), although each L_i will not be observable. Only the awarded amount $(1 + \varepsilon)L_i$ is observed. Of course, if the ε are perfectly correlated between individuals, one can "back out" the value of L_i at the end of the year, when all of the award data are known. However, unlike a price index, the IALA index would only be determinable from the awards themselves (i.e., only from the indemnifiable claims), whereas, for example, a price index on auto parts would be able to use a broader set of market data unrelated to the insurable events.

Optimal contracting is achieved if the insurer covers the full loss, $(1 + \varepsilon)L_i$, but allows for a participating policy whereby the insured leaves the insurer with $1 - \beta^*$ of the ε risk. The participating dividend (which is negative, in the form of an assessment) is calculated after the end of the policy period, when the market has enough data to determine the IALA index. The insurer's share of the ε risk is once again (essentially) nonrandom and deterministic. Indeed, even though one cannot observe each L_i directly at the time the award is made, the insurer is assumed to know the value of EL_i *ex ante*. Therefore, the insurer can turn to the marketplace to hedge its aggregate ε risk.

Of course, the IALA is nothing more than a "wish-list item" for insurers at the moment, as is any market for derivatives on this index, should this index become a reality. However, another potential form of securitization that seems to be gaining some interest in the insurance world is the packaging of standardized risk units for direct sale to the public. A packaging of homogeneous risks, of a size sufficient to eliminate the average idiosyncratic risk component, would leave the purchaser(s) with only the ε risk. Since this risk would not be perfectly correlated with other market indexes (otherwise these

---

[16] See Doherty (1991) for a more complete discussion of the many complicated effects involved. Also, see item "Insurance for Natural Catastrophes" ahead for a discussion on how one might model correlated likelihoods.

indexes could be used themselves to construct a hedge device), it should obtain a price in the marketplace, so long as the IALA, or some similar index, is verifiable.

Once again, the assumption that the ε_i are perfectly correlated is likely to be too strong to fit reality. If the correlation is high enough, this will only mean that the "packaged" liability losses, which contain (essentially) only ε risk in theory, will also contain some type of noise in the aggregate of the ε components, which can once again be treated as a type of basis risk. If the correlations are not high enough, the IALA will be too uninformative, and market-hedging strategies will not be effective. One way to make them more effective would be to define narrower classes of liability risks, ones within which the ε risks are highly correlated. Indeed, insurers currently seem to be in the process of developing liability policies within more and more specialized areas (see Hofmann, 1996). The reason is only partly demand driven, as existing products could easily be marketed to larger classes of insureds. But rather than just attracting new customers for existing products, insurers are continually developing newer product classes, especially in the area of professional liability. Modern databases can be readily fine-tuned to keep track of losses, making specialized versions of an IALA index feasible. Since one assumes here that the ε risks *across* the differing classes of liability risks are not perfectly correlated, insurers can diversify partly by taking separate positions in the various types of liability classes. With more narrowly defined classes, reinsurers become a potential source for diversifying the various types of ε risk, in addition to securitization for direct sale to the public.

Insurance for Natural Catastrophes

As a final example, consider homeowner's insurance for people living in an area exposed to natural catastrophes, such as earthquakes in California or hurricanes in Florida. Indexes of catastrophe losses within such regions are now available. Catastrophe risk, such as hurricane or earthquake risk, commonly exposes those living within a fairly confined area to simultaneous losses. The standard model of variable participation contracts herein seems to fit this scenario fairly well. However, the catastrophic effects are modeled a bit differently here to exhibit how this model can be extended to handle frequency risk correlations. Although severities of losses also are likely to be affected, the authors focus only on the likelihood and assume that individuals possess loss severity distributions L_i that are independent and identically distributed and are conditional on suffering a catastrophic loss.[17]

In reality, policies typically cover a broad range of losses, so that the losses are separated off due to the potentially catastrophic peril. For example, although hurricane damage is covered under typical homeowner's insurance, one can separate out the windstorm peril for the case of hurricanes, as was recently done for blocks of policies in the State of Florida. Let L_i denote the severity distribution conditional upon hurricane damage.

Correlation enters this model via the probability of damage. Let p_0 denote the long-term probability that a particular insured suffers a loss due to a catastrophic event.

---

[17] In a related article, Schlesinger (1999) provided some details of modeling loss severity correlations. He also provided a few numerical examples for interested readers. An extension by Loubergé and Schlesinger (2000) examined the interaction of severity correlation and frequency correlation. The authors provide the frequency risk analysis herein as a building block for these models as well as for future research.

Assume that the group of insureds is defined such that the current-year probability of damage is identical for all insureds. One thus can view p_0 as the relative frequency of losses in an average year. Define δ_i to be a Bernoulli random variable taking on the value 1 with probability $\xi \equiv p_0(1 + \varepsilon)$ and taking on the value zero with probability $1 - \xi$. Maintain all previous assumptions about ε except that one now requires the support of ε to be restricted such that $0 < \xi < 1$. Assume that ξ is identical for all insureds.

One can view p_0 as representing the expected proportion of homeowners who suffer damage from the "catastrophic peril" in a typical year, and view $\xi \equiv p_0(1 + \varepsilon)$ as the random proportion of homeowners suffering damage in the current year. Note that ξ is the true probability that a randomly chosen homeowner suffered a loss in a given year, which is only known as a relative frequency *ex post*. This is *not* to be confused with Bayesian updating. The *ex ante* probability of loss is still viewed as p_0. So, for example, suppose $p_0 = 0.10$ and that this year $\varepsilon = 0.50$. Then the insurer typically would see 10 percent of insured homes suffer a loss from the catastrophic peril. This is a long-term average frequency that includes both catastrophic and noncatastrophic years. However, the current year would see 50 percent more loss claims; i.e., a total of 15 percent of the insured properties would experience losses.

The δ_i are assumed to be independent and identically distributed within the insured group. Under these assumptions, the catastrophe risk held by each individual insured is given by $\delta_i L_i$. Although the individual $\delta_i L_i$ are all independent, the probability ξ is perfectly correlated among all individuals in the insured group. From the insurer's perspective, the *ex ante* risk per policyowner under full nonparticipating insurance is (essentially) $\xi EL \equiv p_0 EL(1 + \varepsilon)$. Since p_0 is a constant, this structure is identical to the multiplicative risk structure presented earlier in this article. Allowing for policy participation, the insurance premium is as given in Equation (6), with the exception that $p_0 EL$ replaces EL. The insured's wealth Y is thus

$$Y = W - \alpha p_0 EL - (1 - \alpha)\delta_i L_i - \alpha p_0 EL[\beta\lambda + (1 - \beta)\varepsilon]. \tag{11}$$

Note that Equation (11) is identical to Equation (7), with the random loss L replaced by $\delta_i L_i$, which in itself yields $E(\delta_i L_i) = p_0 EL$ in place of EL. As a result, the optimal variable participation contract is one for which $\alpha^* = 1$ and $\beta^* = b^*$, where b^* is the optimal hedge on $p_0 EL$ "units" of ε risk for an individual's personal account, if there were some type of market to hedge the ε risk directly. However, the problem here is trickier, since the ε risk is not monetary but probabilistic.

For the insurer, barring transaction costs, it really does not matter financially whether an ε of 0.50 represents the same number of losses, each 50 percent higher in magnitude, or an ε of 0.50 represents losses of the same average magnitude, but 50 percent more of them. At the individual level, rather than now having everyone with a 50 percent higher loss, 50 percent more of the individuals experience a loss. This makes it practically impossible to "undo" the ε effect at the individual level. In the case where the frequency is correlated, one can only undo the ε effect by randomly choosing 50 percent of households experiencing a loss and not paying them any indemnity. Although it might be possible to pay each household an indemnity that is 50 percent lower, this approach could cause problems for cases when $\varepsilon < 0$, when indemnities might need to exceed loss values. These types of problems need not be dealt with, however, since the individual may simply purchase a variable participation contract and let the insurer be the one who turns to the use of securitized products.[18]

Once again, the use of such securitization depends upon ε being well defined. Although long-term probability projections for catastrophes still have not been perfected, much progress has been made. Certainly, the realized value of ε is calculable *ex post*, so long as one agrees on a projected value p_0. The choices available to insurers for hedging the ε risk are growing rapidly. For example, an insurer can trade its ε risk for one type of catastrophe with the ε risk from a different insurer on a different type of catastrophe exposure. Such trades currently exist in the form of "CAT swaps." For example, an insurer in Florida may swap some of its hurricane risk in exchange for taking on some earthquake risk from a California insurer. Alternatively, an insurer can turn to the CBOT for options and futures on catastrophic loss indexes. Although trading volume to date at the CBOT in the area of insurance futures and options has been relatively light, insurers are just beginning to understand and recognize the potential hedging possibilities. Another possible course of action is for the insurer to issue CAT bonds, with a trigger set for the relevant catastrophe event. Of course, for hedging to be effective, the ε risk must be well defined and must be highly correlated within the insured group.[19]

One must be careful at this point to warn the reader that modeling the ε distribution accurately, along with an ability to observe the realized value of ε *ex post*, does not relieve us of the multitude of problems that may be associated with catastrophic risks. For example, in cases where the distribution of ε is heavily skewed, one may run into problems associated with extreme values.[20] This decomposition neither simplifies nor complicates the problems associated with estimating the overall loss distribution. This would be critical, for example, if one wished to develop a method for ascribing the appropriate insurance premia or for performing value-at-risk analyses. Indeed, the ε risk in this model needs to be determined by decomposing the estimated loss distribution.

The goal in this article is not to estimate the tail of the loss distribution but to point out how risk decomposition can aid in the design of better-performing insurance contracts. Such long tails in this model could lead to either extremely high values for the price of risk, γ, or even to the nonexistence of markets for the ε risk. Thus, the contracts

---

[18] See Schlesinger (1999) for further discussion of the details of this case.

[19] Recently, new catastrophe indexes from Property Claims Services (PCS) have been added to those already in use (which uses data from the Insurance Services Office) to extend the product line offered by the CBOT. Obviously, the CBOT agrees with this assessment, that securitization is still developing in the marketplace. Moreover, other exchanges are coming into existence. For example, the newly opened Bermuda Commodities Exchange (BCOE) trades options contracts on certain "atmospheric perils," such as tornadoes, hurricanes, and hailstorms, for specified regions within the United States. The contracts are based on a new index developed by a subsidiary of Guy Carpenter, and bidding takes place over the Internet.

[20] See Embrechts, Klüppelberg, and Mikosch (1997) for an excellent analysis of the multitude of problems involved in modeling long tails with extreme values. Another limitation in this model for dealing with extreme values is that the authors use the simplicity of proportional coverages, rather than the types of stop-loss contracts typically associated with such skewed distributions.

proposed in this model are best viewed as another tool for dealing with catastrophic risks, and not as any type of overall solution.

CONCLUSION

Since securitization is only now beginning to emerge as a viable risk-sharing technique for insurable losses, this model should be viewed as normative. Securitization may evolve through alternative means. If individuals must insure the noncorrelated (idiosyncratic) component of their loss exposure through a nonparticipating insurance contract, then securitized products may develop to allow the individual to directly hedge the correlated (systemic) risk component. Although this is theoretically simple to do in the case of additive risk components, markets for both of the above risk components have not yet shown any indication of evolving in real-world markets, as far as the authors know. For the case of multiplicative risk components, such a hedging strategy is unlikely, due to the random amount of systemic risk attributable to each individual. More likely, and what is seen developing to date, is that securitized products are used directly by insurers. These insurers can then offer "variable participation policies" to individual insureds and pass off any desired amount of the systemic risk, which is not assumed by the policyholders, in the capital market. One sees signs here of a burgeoning market for securitized products.

The efficacy of securitization depends crucially on the separability of the systemic and idiosyncratic risk components and on strong correlations within the systemic component. Recent designs of insurance products and insurance indexes to fit narrower bands of loss exposures with seemingly highly correlated systemic components indicate that the market is indeed developing in this way. This pattern is already appearing with insurers purchasing a growing number of different catastrophe options and futures at the CBOT. Moreover, the systemic component might itself be directly traded, such as is the case with CAT swaps. It also can be hedged via contingencies in debt and/or equity instruments. For instance, the insurer can issue CAT bonds, in which the hedge takes the form of a "forgiveness option" built into a debt issue made by the insurer, or it can issue "cataputs," which are essentially put options in which the insurer can sell new equity at a predetermined price.

Although the authors have not examined the issue in this article, the emergence of a market for securitized products must also obviously relate to transaction costs and/or contracting costs.[21] Perhaps the most apparent saving lies in a reduction in the costs of financial distress to insurers. This is dramatically seen in catastrophe risk. A $50 billion hurricane or earthquake loss in the United States represents about one quarter of the net worth of the entire domestic property-liability insurance industry. Such magnitudes of losses are not unfathomable. For instance, some estimates put the damage done during the 1995 Kobe earthquake in Japan at $100 billion.[22] Moreover, the events of September 11, 2001, have shown that man-made catastrophes can also be quite

---

[21] This is the main focus of a recent article by Froot (2001).

[22] Although the damages were high, the amount of damages insured was only approximately $3 billion, according to data from Munich Reinsurance (see http://www.munichre.de). Munich Reinsurance also predicts that the maximum damage from a single California earthquake could be as high as $150 billion.

severe, with losses of over $100 billion and insurance losses and projected insurance payouts somewhere between $35 and $70 billion.[23]

The prospect of such high losses creates significant costs in terms of both incentive conflicts between stakeholders and potential bankruptcy costs. Yet such losses are small compared with the $20 trillion U.S. capital market. Moreover, since such losses exhibit close to zero correlation with most financial market indexes, the required rate of return for capital market investors should eventually move closer to the risk-free rate as markets develop and become more familiar to insurers and to investors. As insurers have increasingly more tools to decompose and hedge the components of their risks, some simple changes in primary insurance contracts, such as those proposed herein, will allow for more flexible risk management on the part of insureds. It will be interesting to see exactly how the market develops in the years to come. Hopefully, many of these conjectures will prove true. At the very least, the authors hope to stimulate thought within the academic and business worlds on how this topic might be approached.

REFERENCES

Borch, K., 1962, Equilibrium in a Reinsurance Market, *Econometrica*, 30: 424-444.

Cummins, D., N. Doherty, and A. Lo, 2001, Can Insurers Pay for "The Big One?" Measuring the Capacity of an Insurance Market to Respond to Catastrophic Losses, *Journal of Banking and Finance*, forthcoming.

Cummins, D., and M. Weiss, 2000, The Global Market for Reinsurance: Consolidation, Capacity, and Efficiency, *Brookings-Wharton Papers on Financial Services*, R.E. Litan and A.M. Santomero, eds. (Washington, DC: The Brookings Institution), 159-222.

Dionne, G., and N. A. Doherty, 1993, Insurance With Undiversifiable Risk, *Journal of Risk and Uncertainty*, 6: 187-203.

Doherty, N. A., 1991, The Design of Insurance Contracts When Liability Rules Are Unstable, *Journal of Risk and Insurance*, 58: 227-246.

Doherty, N. A., 1997, Financial Innovation in the Management of Catastrophe Risk, *Journal of Applied Corporate Finance*, Fall.

Doherty, N. A., and H. Schlesinger, 1983, Optimal Insurance in Incomplete Markets, *Journal of Political Economy*, 91: 1045-1054.

Embrechts, P., C. Klüppelberg, and T. Mikosch, 1997, *Modeling Extremal Events for Insurance and Finance* (Berlin: Springer-Verlag).

Froot, K. A., 2001, The Market for Catastrophe Risk: A Clinical Examination, *Journal of Financial Economics*, 60: 529-571.

Hofmann, M. A., 1996, Insurers Are Trying Harder to Develop Specialized Professional Liability Products, *Business Insurance*, 30: 13ff.

Karni, E., 1995, Non-Expected Utility and the Robustness of the Classical Insurance Paradigm: Discussion, *Geneva Papers on Risk and Insurance Theory*, 20: 51-56.

---

[23] Numbers are based on projections by the New York State Insurance Department and the Insurance Industry, respectively, as reported in the *New York Post*, January 15, 2002.

Loubergé, H., and H. Schlesinger, 2000, Optimal Catastrophe Insurance, Discussion paper no. 7, International Center for Financial Asset Management and Engineering (FAME).

Marshall, J. M., 1974, Insurance Theory: Reserves Versus Mutuality, *Economic Inquiry*, 12: 476-492.

Machina, M. J., 1982, "Expected Utility" Analysis Without the Independence Axiom, *Econometrica*, 50: 277-323.

Machina, M. J., 1995, Non-Expected Utility and the Robustness of the Classical Insurance Paradigm, *Geneva Papers on Risk and Insurance Theory*, 20: 9-50.

Niehaus, G., and S. Mann, 1992, The Trading of Underwriting Risk: An Analysis of Insurance Futures Contracts and Reinsurance, *Journal of Risk and Insurance*, 59: 601-627.

Quiggin, J., 1982, A Theory of Anticipated Utility, *Journal of Economic Behavior and Organization*, 3: 323-343.

Rothschild, M., and J. Stiglitz, 1970, Increasing Risk: I. A Definition, *Journal of Economic Theory*, 2: 225-243.

Schlesinger, H., 1997, The Demand for Insurance Without the Expected-Utility Paradigm, *Journal of Risk and Insurance*, 64: 19-39.

Schlesinger, H., 1999, Decomposing Catastrophic Risk, *Insurance: Mathematics and Economics*, 24: 95-101.

Segal, U., and A. Spivak, 1990, First Order Versus Second Order Risk Aversion, *Journal of Economic Theory*, 51: 111-125.

Smith, B., and M. Stultzer, 1990, Adverse Selection, Aggregate Uncertainty, and the Role for Mutual Insurance Contracts, *Journal of Business*, 63: 493-510.

Yaari, M. E., 1987, The Dual Theory of Choice Under Risk, *Econometrica*, 55: 95-116.

Zilcha, I., and S. H. Chew, 1990, Invariance of the Efficient Sets When the Expected Utility Hypothesis Is Relaxed, *Journal of Economic Behavior and Organization*, 13: 125-131.

©The Journal of Risk and Insurance, 2002, Vol. 69, No. 1, 63-91

Life Insurance Liabilities at Market Value: An Analysis of Insolvency Risk, Bonus Policy, and Regulatory Intervention Rules in a Barrier Option Framework

Anders Grosen
Peter Løchte Jørgensen

Abstract

This article takes a contingent claim approach to the market valuation of equity and liabilities in life insurance companies. A model is presented that explicitly takes into account the following: (i) the holders of life insurance contracts (LICs) have the first claim on the company's assets, whereas equity holders have limited liability; (ii) interest rate guarantees are common elements of LICs; and (iii) LICs according to the so-called contribution principle are entitled to receive a fair share of any investment surplus. Furthermore, a regulatory mechanism in the form of an intervention rule is built into the model. This mechanism is shown to significantly reduce the insolvency risk of the issued contracts, and it implies that the various claims on the company's assets become more exotic and obtain barrier option properties. Closed valuation formulas are nevertheless derived. Finally, some representative numerical examples illustrate how the model can be used to establish the set of initially fair contracts and to determine the market values of contracts after their inception.

The authors are grateful for helpful comments and suggestions from two anonymous referees; David F. Babbel; Ken L. Bechmann; Zvi Bodie; Peter Ove Christensen; Johannes Raaballe; participants at the 2001 OECD Pension Research Seminar in Sofia, Bulgaria; the 2001 HERMES/University of Cyprus Conference on Asset and Liability Management, Nicosia, Cyprus; the 2001 Danske Bank Seminar on Credit Risk, Middelfart, Denmark; and from participants at workshops at the Copenhagen Business School, Aarhus School of Business, Odense University, and the University of Copenhagen. Any remaining errors are the authors' own responsibility. Financial support from the Danish Natural and Social Science Research Councils and the Centre for Analytical Finance at the University of Aarhus is gratefully acknowledged.

INTRODUCTION

The subject of fair valuation of life insurance liabilities has attracted a lot of attention in the insurance and finance literature in recent years. This is caused by the product structure of the life insurance business as well as certain events in the financial markets.

The late 1980s through the 1990s was a period of quite some turmoil for the life insurance business, and Europe, Japan, and the United States can all present their own spectacularly long lists of defaulted life insurance companies. Many of these were relatively small, but some massive defaults of large economic significance also occurred including the United States' First Executive Corporation ($19 billion in assets), France's Garantie Mutuelle des Functionnaires (see Briys and de Varenne, 1994), and Nissan Mutual Life of Japan, which went bankrupt with uncovered liabilities of $2.56 billion (see Grosen and Jørgensen, 2000).

In retrospective discussions of the reasons for these unfortunate events, three issues appear repeatedly. The first is the mismanagement of the interest rate guarantees issued with most life insurance policies. The second is the mismanagement of credit risk stemming from either side of the balance sheet, and the third relates to the application of poor or inappropriate accounting principles, which in many cases have critically delayed or suppressed potentially useful warning signs in relation to company solvency. These issues are, of course, closely interrelated, as will be further clarified in the subsequent discussion.

The focus on the interest rate guarantee relates to the fact that most policies contain an explicit guarantee that the holder's account will be credited—on a year-to-year basis—with a rate of return (the *policy interest rate*) of at least some fixed guaranteed rate, say, 5 percent. At the time of issuance, the guaranteed interest rate has typically been (much) lower than prevailing market interest rates, a fact that has led companies to ignore their value (as well as their risk), and, to the best of the authors' knowledge, premiums for these issued guarantees (read: liabilities) have not been demanded anywhere before 1999.[1] However, as a result of a period when market interest rates have generally been declining and when guaranteed interest rates have been held fixed, the companies have experienced a dramatic narrowing in the safety margin between the earning power of their assets and the claims from issued liabilities. This particular development is a major source of the problems of some life insurance companies, although it is also a bit ironic, because the fundamental function of insurance companies in general is to provide a guaranty of asset value to the customer, as pointed out by, e.g., Merton and Bodie (1992). Interest rate guarantees are thus a source of credit risk arising from the liability side of the balance sheet.

The regulatory authorities in Japan as well as in the EU countries have responded to the threat of insolvency from the return guarantees by lowering the maximum interest rate

---

[1] In 1999, the largest Danish life insurance company, Danica, introduced an annual premium for the interest rate guarantees issued at the highest level, 4.5 percent. The premium amounted to 0.5 percent of the life insurance liabilities. Another Danish company, Skandia Liv, has introduced annual charges of 0.27 and 0.17 percent for contracts issued with interest rate guarantees of 4.5 and 2.5 percent, respectively.

TABLE 1

Country	Maximum Rates as of July 1, 2000	Previous Maximum Rates
U.S.A.	None	-
Japan	2.50%	4.50% before 1997
Austria	3.25%	4.00% until July 1, 2000
Belgium	3.75%	4.75% until January 1, 1999
Denmark	2.00%	5.00% until July 1, 1994
		3.00% until January 1, 1999
France	2.75%	3.75% until January 1, 1998
Germany	3.25%	4.00% until July 1, 2000
Hungary	5.50%[a]	
Italy	3.00%	
Luxembourg	2.75%	3.75% before 1998
Netherlands	3.00%	4.00% before 1998
Norway	3.00%	4.00%[b]
Portugal	4.00%	
Spain	3.20%	4.00% until June 21, 1997
Sweden	3.00%	4.00% before 1998
Turkey	9.00%/2.50%[c]	
United Kingdom	rules on the way	

The information in this table is compiled from a number of sources, the most important of which is *Survey on the Rating of the Principal Categories of Individual Life Insurance Contracts*, Comité Européen des Assurances, October 1998. The entire material is available from the authors on request.
[a] Reduction on the way.
[b] For some older contracts.
[c] For national and hard currency–based contracts, respectively.

that can legally be guaranteed to policyholders.[2] Table 1 illustrates this development by showing the level of the prevalent maximum *technical rates*, the previous maximum rates, and some (approximate) dates of recent reductions for the EU member countries, Japan, and a few other countries.

These regulatory initiatives have forced companies to lower the guaranteed rates for new contracts. Consequently, life insurance companies commonly have (cohorts of) policies with different guaranteed rates in the same fund. This raises the question of how to avoid inequitable treatment of the different classes of policyholders. The common, "easy-way-out" approach of attempting to credit all policies with an identical rate that is higher than or equal to the largest guaranteed rate in the fund may

---

[2] Specifically, Article 18 of the Third EU Life Insurance Directive, which was effective as of November 10, 1992, requires that interest rate guarantees do not exceed 60 percent of the rate of return on government debt (of unspecified maturity).

very well enhance the default risk of a business that is already in trouble. Clearly, the correct route to a fair distribution of surplus among a family of unequal claims goes via a market valuation of the various claims—an issue that will be addressed further herein as a key objective of the article.

In relation to the market valuation of life insurance liabilities, it is also worth noting that initiatives have been taken by the insurance business itself as well as by the accounting profession. In 1994, for example, the American Academy of Actuaries appointed a Fair Valuation of Liabilities Task Force to consider the problems associated with the measurement of fair value (see, e.g., Babbel and Merrill, 1998, and Babbel and Merrill, 1999). The Task Force report is contained in Vanderhoof and Altman (1998) along with several other significant contributions to the understanding of the fair value of insurance liabilities. The Financial Accounting Standards Board (FASB) has also addressed the problem of market value accounting by issuing a series of *statements of standards* concerning derivative financial instruments in general (e.g., FAS 107, 115, 119, 133, and 137) and life insurance liabilities in particular (FAS 120).[3] In addition, the International Accounting Standard Committee (IASC) has launched a project to develop an international Generally Accepted Accounting Principle for insurers that can be accepted by stock markets, regulators, and the insurance industry. See Forfar and Masters (1999) for a more detailed discussion of the present work toward developing international accounting standards for the life insurance business. The IASC Steering Committee is expected to publish the International Accounting Standard in fall 2002.

The above-mentioned initiatives can be interpreted as evidence of increased acceptance and understanding of the fact that interest rate guarantees (as one among sometimes many embedded options in life insurance contracts) are liabilities to the issuer.[4] Such issued options represent valuable obligations and constitute potential hazards to company solvency, and they should therefore be included in a proper valuation of the liabilities (see also discussions later in this article). Historically, this has not been done. The FASB and IASC initiatives represent tremendous potential for improving the transparency of the accounts of life insurance companies. In particular, mark-to-market accounting can more than likely serve as the basis of a better early-warning system than the ancient accounting systems based on book values (i.e., amortized acquisition cost) and/or historical values. The opportunities for monitoring by shareholders, policyholders, and regulatory authorities should also inevitably be enhanced.[5] The effective monitoring and regulation of a life insurance company for which market values of all elements of the balance sheet can be established is another key objective of this article.

---

[3] FAS 120 is entitled *Accounting and Reporting by Mutual Life Insurance Enterprises and by Insurance Enterprises for Certain Long-Duration Participating Contracts.*

[4] See Smith (1982) for an early study of the life insurance policy as an options package and for a discussion of problems caused by statutory accounting principles in relation to the insolvency issue. Babbel (1994) contains some interesting views on the implications of fair value reporting.

[5] This has, in part, motivated that market value accounting combined with exposure or risk accounting is enforced by law for all life insurance companies in Denmark beginning in 2002.

This article has been motivated by the issues discussed above. A stylized, dynamic model will be set up for a life insurance company in which the issues of the interest rate guarantees, insolvency risk, and market valuation of the balance sheet elements as well as some additional issues can be handled. The liability and equity contracts will be priced and analyzed as financial economists deal with contingent claims; i.e., the rich toolbox of contingent claims analysis, e.g., no-arbitrage and martingale pricing techniques, will be used. The authors are obviously not the first to take this approach, and a discussion of related literature will clarify where contributions from this article lie.

Brennan and Schwartz (1976), Boyle and Schwartz (1977), and Brennan and Schwartz (1979) were the first articles that elegantly described some of the option elements of life insurance products and demonstrated how the then relatively young option pricing theory of Black and Scholes (1973) could be applied to value these contracts. The contracts considered in the above-mentioned articles were so-called unit-linked contracts without credit risk and with option elements of European type.[6] Baccinello and Ortu (1993b), Grosen and Jørgensen (1997), and Nielsen and Sandmann (1995) represent other, more recent papers that all analyze some form of unit-linked contracts. For example, Grosen and Jørgensen (1997) establish arbitrage-free prices of unit-linked contracts with a return guarantee and the American-style option to exercise prematurely by applying results from American option pricing theory. They also point out that the value of the option to exercise prematurely is precisely the value of the surrender option implicit in many life insurance contracts.

However elegant, the concentration of articles analyzing unit-linked policies is in sharp contrast to the economic significance of these products in the insurance market, where so-called participating (or with U.K. terminology, *with profits*) policies are by far the most important. Participating policies allow the holders to participate in upside returns, as the policies may receive bonuses in addition to the promised payments implied by the interest rate guarantee. The issue of describing and analyzing the bonus distribution mechanism is highly complex,[7] which undoubtedly explains why so few articles have dealt with this issue. However, interest has increased in unveiling the structure of these mechanisms and in analyzing participating policies, as documented by Miltersen and Persson (1998), Briys and de Varenne (1994), Briys and de Varenne (1997), Grosen and Jørgensen (2000), and Jensen et al. (2001). In particular, the model by Briys and de Varenne (1994, 1997) (henceforth the BV model) contains a participation mechanism and distinguishes itself by taking the credit risk of the issuer explicitly into account in the valuation of the insureds' claims.[8]

The principle underlying the BV model is Merton's (Merton, 1974, 1977, 1978, 1989) option pricing approach to the valuation of corporate debt, deposit insurance, and financial intermediaries. Following Merton, Briys and de Varenne introduced the

---

[6] A policy is unit-linked (equity-linked) if the interest rate credited to the customer's account is linked directly and without lags to the return on some reference (equity) portfolio—the *unit*.

[7] See the discussion in Grosen and Jørgensen (2000).

[8] The credit risk of the insurer has been addressed in other articles but from the point of view of a (government) guarantor who is obliged to make the promised payments of the contract if the insurer fails to do so; see, e.g., Kalra and Jain (1997) and Han, Lai, and Witt (1997).

default risk of the insurer as a put option arising from the limited liability enjoyed by equity holders when the insurer issues debt, i.e., insurance policies. The option is of European type, and if at the date of maturity the company is unable to meet the insureds' demands, the shareholders simply walk away. Hence, equity holders do not incur all the downside costs of default while capturing some of the upside earnings. Because of this asymmetric payoff, the insolvency put option increases in value as the insurer takes on more risk.

This article takes the BV model as its point of departure; the reason is threefold. First, the BV framework is well-known, and the model was one of the first to take the credit risk of the insurer into account in the economic valuation of insurance liabilities. Second, the simplicity of the bonus distribution mechanism in the BV model allows one to derive closed formulas for contract values and to easily perform various sensitivity analyses even after significantly extending the model. Third, despite the simplifications in the bonus distribution mechanism, the BV model remains a fairly good proxy for the different kind of interest rate guarantees embedded in life insurance contracts across countries and types of contracts. In this last respect, time may in fact work *for* the BV model in the sense that the interest rate guarantees embedded in life insurance contracts presently seem to be subject to redesign in many countries. This is happening as a response to the potential insolvency problems induced by the previously common design in which the guaranteed minimum annual return implied a binding floor under the cash values of contracts that was ratcheted upward each time profits were shared with contract holders. In Denmark, for example, many insurance companies are now changing their distribution mechanism from the above-mentioned *ratcheting system* to a mechanism that implies what is referred to as *conditional bonus* and that is very similar to the system modeled by Briys and de Varenne (1997).

However, a significant weakness of the BV model is that it evaluates stakeholders' claims and detects bankruptcy only at the maturity date. Despite its formulation in continuous time, it is essentially a single-period model in which a dynamic element of the insolvency put option is lost and, perhaps more important, the built-in interest rate guarantee serves no specific purpose, as it is indistinguishable from an absolute maturity guarantee (see the discussions in Boyle and Hardy, 1997, and Grosen and Jørgensen, 2000). The authors aim to correct this weakness and reintroduce the dynamic element to the BV model by imposing a certain regulatory restriction that assumes continuous monitoring of the solvency of the firm and a closure rule based on the nominal liability implied by the interest rate guarantee. This extension opens for a wide range of interesting analyses in relation to the issues discussed earlier in this introduction.

The cost of adding realism to the model in this way will be increased complexity of the options involved. More specifically, the stakeholders' claims will change from plain vanilla options to more exotic option types with features similar to so-called financial knockout barrier options. Luckily, the possibility of deriving closed formulas is not destroyed by this extension. The authors establish these rather complex formulas, which are interesting in themselves, from an option theorist's point of view and implement them to provide a sample of illustrative numerical examples.

The rest of the paper is organized as follows. "Model Basics" is followed by "Conract Specifications," in which the details of the various contracts and the regulatory mechanism are explained. Pricing formulas for the contracts are presented in the "Valuation" section (derivations are in the Appendix). These formulas are implemented in "Implementation and Numerical Examples," which also contains a wide variety of illustrative, representative examples. The final section contains our conclusions as well as some suggestions for future research.

MODEL BASICS

In this section, the model is introduced that will be used to analyze the aspects of the life insurance products discussed in the Introduction. After a brief presentation of some basics, the authors will describe the precise characteristics of the various model claims and then present a dynamic framework for the valuation of these claims.

The basic framework is inspired by Briys and de Varenne (1997) and is as follows. Agents are assumed to operate in a continuous-time frictionless economy with a perfect financial market, so that tax effects, transaction costs, divisibility, liquidity, short sales constraints, and other imperfections can be ignored.

The financial arrangement of interest for analysis is initiated at time zero, where two (groups of) agents—policyholders and equity holders—agree on forming a mutual company, the life insurance company.[9] The two agents each invest a sum of money in the company whereby they form the company's initial asset base, A_0, as illustrated by the time zero balance sheet below in Figure 1, where $L_0 \equiv \alpha A_0$ is the initial investment by the policyholders and where $E_0 \equiv (1 - \alpha)A_0$ is the initial investment by the equity holders. The parameter α is referred to as the *wealth distribution coefficient*.

By their initial investments, the agents acquire a claim for a payoff on or before the maturity date T. As will shortly become clear, these claims are very similar to financial derivatives, with the company's assets as the well-defined underlying asset. Hence, given a precise description of the various claim characteristics, one can first price the balance sheet elements using the powerful apparatus of contingent claims valuation. Second, and perhaps more important, with the valuation formulas in hand one can explore and describe combinations of contract characteristics (parameters) and initial investment amounts, which lead to fair distribution of value in the sense that initial investments equal the time zero market value of the associated contingent claims.

FIGURE 1

Assets	Liabilities
A_0	$L_0 \equiv \alpha A_0$
	$E_0 \equiv (1 - \alpha)A_0$
A_0	A_0

---

[9] It is natural to think of the first type of agents as buying a policy from the company and as the second type of agents as residual claimants and, hence, as policyholders and equity holders, respectively.

While one would naturally assume that all contracts are initiated at fair terms, it should be realized that as soon as contract terms are fixed and time passes, changes in the underlying variable (total assets) will inevitably be observed. This will lead to changes in the market values of the balance sheet elements and to a redistribution of wealth between policyholders and equity holders. In a world where accounting practices and legislation are changing toward demanding market values in accounting statements (See the Introduction), models that can determine these values at all times and in all states of the economy will be important. This article should be seen as an attempt to construct such a model.

CONTRACT SPECIFICATIONS

This section describes the details of the stakeholders' claims on the company's assets, beginning with a specification of the liability holders' claim.[10]

The Liability Holders' Claim

As discussed in the Introduction, most life insurance policies contain an explicit interest rate guarantee, i.e., a guarantee that the invested funds will accumulate by at least some preset, fixed rate. In the terminology herein, this means that the company promises the policyholders a continuously compounded return on the initial market value of the liabilities of at least r_G during the life of the contract. This translates into a guaranteed final payment of $L_T^G = L_0 \cdot e^{r_G T}$. In this connection, two observations are in order. First, as the absence of an external guarantor is assumed, the company's promise can be honored only if it turns out that $A_T > L_T^G$ at time T. In the opposite case, $A_T \leq L_T^G$, and in the event that the company has not been prematurely shut down by regulators, the policyholders receive A_T and leave the equity holders with nothing. Second, note that if there are neither intermediate cash flows nor regulatory evaluations (audits) of the company between time 0 and T, then the return guarantee introduced earlier is exactly equivalent to a simple maturity guarantee for some fixed dollar amount, as analyzed in Merton's classic article (Merton, 1974). In other words, in order for return guarantees to play a nontrivial role, they must either be used to calculate wealth accumulations to contracts on a period-by-period basis (as in Miltersen and Persson, 1998 and Grosen and Jørgensen, 2000) or be used in the definition of a regulatory benchmark throughout the life of the contract (this will be clarified shortly).[11]

In addition to the promised maturity payment implied by the guaranteed rate of return, policyholders are also generally entitled to receive a bonus if the market value of the assets evolves sufficiently favorably.[12] Recent literature (see the Introduction) has intensely debated how to realistically model this bonus option element of life insurance contracts.[13] Here the authors adopt the approach of Briys and de Varenne

---

[10] The terms *liability holders* and *policyholders* are used interchangeably.

[11] For more on the difference between rate of return guarantees and maturity guarantees, see the discussion in Grosen and Jørgensen (2000).

[12] This rests on the broadly defined *contribution principle* of life insurance. See, e.g., Black and Skipper (1994, p. 608).

[13] See also the general discussion on the (in)efficiency of bonus mechanisms in life insurance in Brennan (1993).

(1997), who, assuming assets are earmarked from the beginning, specified the payoff of the bonus option as

$$\delta[\alpha A_T - L_T^G]^+. \tag{1}$$

From Equation (1) it is clear that in the final states where the policyholders' "share" of total value exceeds the promised payment of L_T^G, they will receive a fraction, δ, of this surplus. The parameter δ models the extent to which the policyholders participate in upside payoffs and is hence denoted as the participation coefficient. Fair values of δ must lie in the interval $[0; 1[$ with $(1-\delta)$ representing—in some sense—payment for the partial downside protection.

To sum up, the total maturity payoff to policyholders, $\Psi_L(A_T)$, can be described as

$$\Psi_L(A_T) = \begin{cases} A_T & A_T < L_T^G \\ L_T^G & L_T^G \leq A_T \leq \frac{L_T^G}{\alpha} \\ L_T^G + \delta[\alpha A_T - L_T^G] & A_T > \frac{L_T^G}{\alpha} \end{cases} \tag{2}$$

or more compactly,

$$\Psi_L(A_T) = \delta[\alpha A_T - L_T^G]^+ + L_T^G - [L_T^G - A_T]^+. \tag{3}$$

The first part of the right-hand side has already been labeled as the bonus option. The two remaining terms correspond to a fixed maturity payment and a shorted put option, respectively, and are hence collectively equivalent to a risky (defaultable) bond payoff.[14] Figure 2 is a graphical illustration of Equation (3).

Equation (3) defines the maturity payoff to the liability holders' contract, and if this was the single possible payoff time of the contract, standard techniques for European-style derivatives could be used for valuation. However, inspired by real-life facts, the authors wish to add a dimension—and hence realism—to the model by imposing a regulatory restriction. Technically, suppose that in the framework above, the options will only be allowed to expire provided that

$$A_t > \lambda L_0 e^{r_G t} \equiv B_t, \quad \forall t \in [0, T[, \tag{4}$$

where the curve $\{B(t)\}_{0 \leq t < T}$ will henceforth be referred to as the regulatory boundary. The interpretation and motivation for this restriction are straightforward: $L_0 e^{r_G t}$ is the policyholders' initial deposit compounded with the guaranteed rate of return up to time t. Therefore, only in the event that the total assets at all times have been sufficient to cover this nominal liability multiplied by some prespecified constant, λ (the boundary level parameter), will the stakeholders' options live through to the date of maturity.

In the opposite event, assets will at some point in time, τ, have assumed a market value such that $A_\tau = B_\tau$. In this situation the market value of the assets is at a critical low, and it is assumed that regulatory authorities close down the company immediately and distribute the recovered wealth to stakeholders.

---

[14] Note that the structure of the payoff function in Equation (3) is also very similar to the payoff of a convertible security, as discussed in Ingersoll (1987, p. 430).

FIGURE 2

Maturity Payoff to Liability Holder

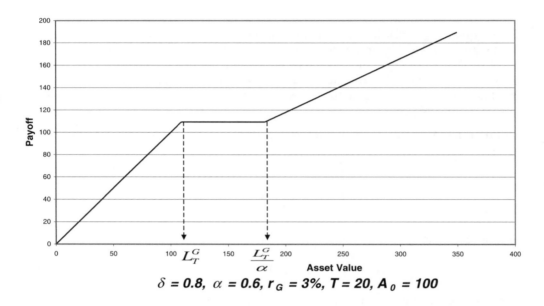

$\delta = 0.8$, $\alpha = 0.6$, $r_G = 3\%$, $T = 20$, $A_0 = 100$

At this point, note that there are two interesting cases. For $\lambda \geq 1$ and in the event of a boundary hit, the trustees will be able to repay to policyholders their initial deposit compounded with the promised rate of return, r_G, up to the closure date. At the same date, a positive surplus of $(\lambda - 1)L_0 e^{r_G \tau}$ can be distributed to either equity holders, regulatory authorities, or other third parties (lawyers). Hence, $\lambda \geq 1$ corresponds to a situation in which regulatory authorities prevent defaults by allowing continued operation solely for companies that have a "buffer" of a certain magnitude between the market value of their assets and the nominal obligations to policyholders. Conversely, $\lambda < 1$ corresponds to a situation in which regulatory authorities allow temporary and limited deficits, and if default is triggered in this situation, the recovered assets will not be sufficient to cover the policyholders' initial deposit compounded with the guaranteed return up to date τ.[15] Assume that policyholders will then be given the entire recovered market value and that equity holders must walk away empty-handed. The various situations are illustrated in Figures 3a and 3b.

With the above-mentioned regulatory restriction imposed, the solution of the model, i.e., the determination of E_0 and L_0, has become considerably more involved. Specifically, the stakeholders' claims have changed from plain vanilla options to more exotic types of options with features in common with so-called financial knockout barrier options. In the proposed setup, the knockout barrier is exponential and defined as the earlier introduced curve $\{B_t\}_{0 \leq t \leq T}$.

---

[15] In particular, note that as $\lambda \downarrow 0$, the model of Briys and de Varenne (1997) is recovered as a special case of this model (see also later in this article). This situation can also be seen as corresponding to total regulatory laxity.

FIGURE 3a
Simulated Asset Values and Exponential Boundaries

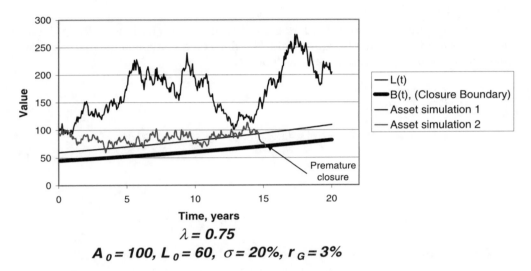

$$\lambda = 0.75$$
$$A_0 = 100, \, L_0 = 60, \, \sigma = 20\%, \, r_G = 3\%$$

FIGURE 3b
Simulated Asset Values and Exponential Boundaries

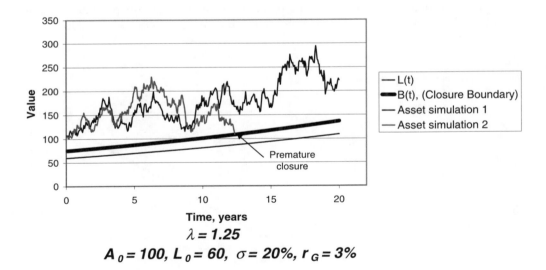

$$\lambda = 1.25$$
$$A_0 = 100, \, L_0 = 60, \, \sigma = 20\%, \, r_G = 3\%$$

As described above, policyholders will be compensated in the event of premature closure at the hitting time τ. Formally, and in accordance with the discussion above, this rebate, $\Theta_L(\tau)$, is given as

$$\Theta_L(\tau) = \begin{cases} L_0 e^{r_G \tau} & \lambda \geq 1 \\ \lambda L_0 e^{r_G \tau} & \lambda < 1 \end{cases} = (\lambda \wedge 1) L_0 e^{r_G \tau}. \tag{5}$$

Before considering the valuation of the composite contingent claim, (Ψ_L, Θ_L), the details regarding the equity holders' claim are described.

The Equity Holders' Claim

The maturity payoff to equity holders is implicit in the discussions in the previous section. As residual claimants, equity holders will receive a payoff at the maturity date conditional on no premature closure as follows:

$$
\Psi_E(A_T) = \begin{cases} 0 & A_T < L_T^G \\ A_T - L_T^G & L_T^G \le A_T \le \frac{L_T^G}{\alpha} \\ A_T - L_T^G - \delta[\alpha A_T - L_T^G] = (1 - \delta)[\alpha A_T - L_T^G] + (1 - \alpha)A_T & A_T > \frac{L_T^G}{\alpha} \end{cases}
$$

(6)

or

$$
\Psi_E(A_T) = [A_T - L_T^G]^+ - \delta[\alpha A_T - L_T^G]^+ = [A_T - L_T^G]^+ - \delta\alpha \left[A_T - \frac{L_T^G}{\alpha} \right]^+ .
$$

(7)

Observe that the payoff to equity holders is the difference between two call options. The long option is simply a call on total assets with an exercise price equal to the promised maturity payment to the liability holders. The shorted call is the bonus option issued to liability holders. This type of payoff function is depicted in Figure 4.

As regards a possible premature closure rebate to equity holders, the previous section established that there could be no such rebate in a regime where $\lambda \le 1$. However,

FIGURE 4
Maturity Payoff to Equity Holder

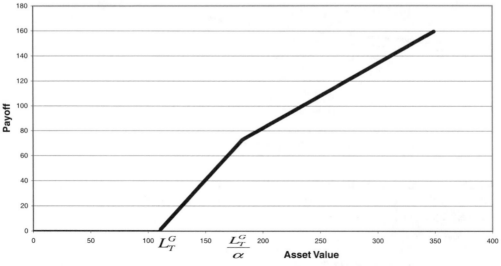

$\delta = 0.8,\ \alpha = 0.6,\ r_G = 3\%,\ T = 20,\ A_0 = 100$

in the case where $\lambda > 1$, there will be a buffer-surplus in the event of closure, which opens the way for a possible premature cash flow to equity holders in the event of a forced closure. An alternative and very reasonable assumption would be that the surplus in this case would go to third parties such as the regulatory authority and/or lawyers. However interesting, this possibility is not explored further in this article, and the rebate to equity holders in the event of premature closure will thus be

$$\Theta_E(\tau) = \begin{cases} (\lambda - 1)L_0 e^{r_G \tau} & \lambda \geq 1 \\ 0 & \lambda < 1 \end{cases} = [(\lambda - 1) \vee 0]L_0 e^{r_G \tau}. \tag{8}$$

VALUATION

With the stakeholders' claims well described, one can now move on to considering the pricing of their various elements, as described above. For this purpose, a dynamic model must be specified for the evolution of the assets through time. The basic framework of Black and Scholes (1973) is adapted, in which all activity occurs on a filtered probability space $(\Omega, \mathcal{F}, (\mathcal{F}_t), P)$ supporting Brownian motion on the finite time interval $[0, T]$. In this setup, the dynamic evolution of the assets is described by the stochastic differential equation

$$dA_t = \xi A_t dt + \sigma A_t dW_t^P, \tag{9}$$

where ξ and σ are positive constants and $\{W_t^P\}$ is a standard Brownian motion under P.[16] Assuming that the riskless interest rate, r, is constant and positive, we have[17]

$$dA_t = r A_t dt + \sigma A_t dW_t^Q, \tag{10}$$

where $\{W_t^Q\}$ is a standard Brownian motion under the familiar equivalent risk-neutral probability measure, Q (see Harrison and Kreps, 1979). Equation (10) defines the well-known geometric Brownian motion, and this particular choice is crucial for the later derivation of closed formulas for the values of the balance sheet elements.[18]

The risk-neutral process and measure are introduced to facilitate valuation by taking advantage of the powerful apparatus of martingale pricing. From this theory (see,

---

[16] The assumption of a constant drift rate in the asset value process is stronger than necessary. The analysis that follows would carry through without changes with a time- and/or state-dependent drift rate.

[17] The assumption of a constant interest rate obviously imposes limitations on the analyses in this article, and the later numerical results should be interpreted with this assumption in mind. The advantage of the assumption is that it allows the derivation of relatively simple closed-form valuation formulas (see later). While it *is* possible to include stochastic interest rates in this setting, such an extension renders highly complex valuation formulas at best, and in the interest of simplicity and since the authors are primarily concerned with studying effects other than those created by a stochastically changing term structure of interest rates, this extension is not discussed herein.

[18] Although most other processes for the asset value evolution would not lead to closed valuation formulas, the properties of the model using alternative processes could still be explored, for example, by means of a Monte Carlo simulation.

e.g.,Björk, 1998), absence of arbitrage implies that under the probability measure Q, all discounted value processes will be martingales. As a direct consequence, letting $V_i(A_t,t)$, $i = L,E$ denote the time t value of the liability holders and equity holders' claims, respectively, write

$$V_i(A_t,t) = e^{-r(T-t)}E_t^Q\{\Psi_i(A_T) \cdot 1_{\{\tau>T\}}\} + E_t^Q\{e^{-r(\tau-t)}\Theta_i(\tau)\}, \tag{11}$$

where E_t^Q denotes expectation with respect to the risk-neutral measure, Q, conditional on time t information; τ is the first-hitting time to the barrier introduced above; and $1_{\mathcal{A}}$ denotes the indicator function on the set $\mathcal{A}$. Note that the first term on the right-hand side of Equation (11) represents the time t value of the contingent maturity payment and that the expectation is made conditional on no premature barrier hit (no forced closure) via the indicator function. The second term represents the time t value of the contingent rebate payment.

One way to proceed from the general valuation expression in Equation (11) would be to manipulate the integrals corresponding to the expectations with appropriate densities inserted. For the first integral, one would require the defective risk-neutral density for the value of the assets at time T with an absorbing barrier $\{B_t\}_{0 \leq t \leq T}$ imposed, and for the second integral one would need the risk-neutral first-hitting time density of A through the absorbing barrier. Establishing these densities and calculating the integrals is a lengthy and tedious exercise that is best omitted here.[19] The resulting valuation formulas appear in the following theorem, and a shorter proof appears in the Appendix that is partly based on recognizing the problems herein as variants of standard knockout barrier option problems, the solution of which can be found in the literature.

Theorem 1: The Value of the Liability Holders' Claim. *The maturity payment to the liability holders conditional on no barrier hit given as $\Psi_L(A_T)$ in Equation (3) is composed of three parts: a bonus (call) option element, a fixed payment, and a shorted put option element. In the event of a premature barrier hit, a rebate payment will be specified by $\Theta_L(\cdot)$ in Equation (5). $V_L(A_t,t)$ is the sum of the time t value of these four separate elements as given below in parts (i)–(iv), where appears the notation*

$$d_\gamma^\pm(x,t) = \frac{\ln(x) + (r - \gamma \pm \frac{1}{2}\sigma^2)(T - t)}{\sigma\sqrt{(T - t)}}, \tag{12}$$

and where $N(\cdot)$ denotes the cumulative standard normal distribution function.

Departing from Equations (3) and (11), one finds (i)–(iii):

---

[19] These details are available from the authors on request.

(i) The time t value of the bonus (call) option element:

$$e^{-r(T-t)}E_t^Q\{\delta[\alpha A_T - L_T^G]^+ \cdot 1_{\{\tau>T\}}\}$$

$$= \delta\alpha\left\{A_t N\left(d_0^+\left(\frac{A_t}{X},t\right)\right) - \frac{L_T^G}{\alpha}e^{-r(T-t)}N\left(d_0^-\left(\frac{A_t}{X},t\right)\right)\right.$$

$$\left.- \left(\frac{A_t}{B_t}\right)^{1-\frac{2(r-r_G)}{\sigma^2}}\left[\frac{B_t^2}{A_t}N\left(d_0^+\left(\frac{B_t^2/A_t}{X},t\right)\right) - \frac{L_T^G}{\alpha}e^{-r(T-t)}N\left(d_0^-\left(\frac{B_t^2/A_t}{X},t\right)\right)\right]\right\},$$

where $X \equiv L_T^G\left(\lambda \vee \frac{1}{\alpha}\right)$.

(ii) The time t value of the conditional fixed payment element:

$$e^{-r(T-t)}E_t^Q\left\{L_T^G \cdot 1_{\{\tau>T\}}\right\}$$

$$= L_T^G e^{-r(T-t)}\left\{N\left(d_{r_G}^-\left(\frac{A_t}{B_t},t\right)\right) - \left(\frac{A_t}{B_t}\right)^{1-\frac{2(r-r_G)}{\sigma^2}}N\left(d_{r_G}^-\left(\frac{B_t}{A_t},t\right)\right)\right\}.$$

(iii) The time t value of the shorted put option element:

$$-1_{\{\lambda<1\}} \cdot e^{-r(T-t)}E_t^Q\left\{[L_T^G - A_T]^+ \cdot 1_{\{\tau>T\}}\right\}$$

$$= -1_{\{\lambda<1\}}\left\{L_T^G e^{-r(T-t)}\left[N\left(-d_0^-\left(\frac{A_t}{L_T^G},t\right)\right) - N\left(-d_{r_G}^-\left(\frac{A_t}{B_t},t\right)\right)\right]\right.$$

$$-A_t\left[N\left(-d_0^+(\frac{A_t}{L_T^G},t)\right) - N\left(-d_{r_G}^+(\frac{A_t}{B_t},t)\right)\right]$$

$$-\left(\frac{A_t}{B_t}\right)^{1-\frac{2(r-r_G)}{\sigma^2}}\left\{L_T^G e^{-r(T-t)}\left[N\left(-d_0^-\left(\frac{B_t^2}{A_t L_T^G},t\right)\right) - N\left(-d_{r_G}^-\left(\frac{B_t}{A_t},t\right)\right)\right]\right.$$

$$\left.\left.-\frac{B_t^2}{A_t}\left[N\left(-d_0^+\left(\frac{B_t^2}{A_t L_T^G},t\right)\right) - N\left(-d_{r_G}^+\left(\frac{B_t}{A_t},t\right)\right)\right]\right\}\right\}.$$

Finally, departing from Equations (5) and (11),

(iv) The time t value of the rebate:

$$E_t^Q\left\{e^{-r(\tau-t)}(\lambda \wedge 1)L_0 e^{r_G\tau}\right\}$$

$$= \frac{(\lambda \wedge 1)}{\lambda}A_t\left\{N\left(-d_{r_G}^+(\frac{A_t}{B_t},t)\right) + \left(\frac{A_t}{B_t}\right)^{-1-\frac{2(r-r_G)}{\sigma^2}}N\left(d_{r_G}^+(\frac{B_t}{A_t},t)\right)\right\}.$$

Proof of Theorem 1: See the Appendix. ■

Theorem 2: The Value of the Equity Holders' Claim. *The maturity payment to the equity holders conditional on no barrier hit given as $\Psi_E(A_T)$ in Equations (6)–(7) is the difference between two call option payoffs: one straight residual claim call option and another call option* *that corresponds precisely to the liability holders' bonus option. In the event of a premature boundary hit, there may be a rebate payment to the equity holders, as specified in Equation (8).*

$V_E(A_t,t)$ *is the sum of the time t value of these three separate elements, as listed below.*

(i) The time t value of the long residual claim (call option) element:

$$e^{-r(T-t)}E_t^Q\left\{[A_T - L_T^G]^+ \cdot 1_{\{\tau > T\}}\right\}$$

$$= A_t N\left(d_0^+\left(\frac{A_t}{Y},t\right)\right) - L_T^G e^{-r(T-t)}N\left(d_0^-\left(\frac{A_t}{Y},t\right)\right)$$

$$- \left(\frac{A_t}{B_t}\right)^{1-\frac{2(r-r_G)}{\sigma^2}}\left[\frac{B_t^2}{A_t}N\left(d_0^+\left(\frac{B_t^2/A_t}{Y},t\right)\right) - L_T^G e^{-r(T-t)}N\left(d_0^-\left(\frac{B_t^2/A_t}{Y},t\right)\right)\right]$$

where $Y \equiv (B_T \vee L_T^G)$.

(ii) The time t value of the shorted bonus option: See part (ii) of Theorem 1.

(iii) The time t value of the equity holders' rebate:

As previously discussed in "The Equity Holders' Claim," a rebate to the equity holders is only a possibility when $\lambda > 1$. Referring to Equation (8), one can thus write

$$E_t^Q\left\{e^{-r(\tau-t)}[(\lambda - 1) \vee 0]L_0 e^{r_G\tau}\right\}$$

$$= \frac{[(\lambda - 1) \vee 0]}{\lambda}A_t\left\{N\left(-d_{r_G}^+\left(\frac{A_t}{B_t},t\right)\right) + \left(\frac{A_t}{B_t}\right)^{-1-\frac{2(r-r_G)}{\sigma^2}}N\left(d_{r_G}^+\left(\frac{B_t}{A_t},t\right)\right)\right\}.$$

Proof of Theorem 2: Part (i) is established by setting $\delta = \alpha = 1$ in part (i) of Theorem 1. Part (ii) is precisely part (i) of Theorem 1 with the sign reversed. Part (iii) rests on calculations similar to those that established part (iv) of Theorem 1. ∎

IMPLEMENTATION AND NUMERICAL EXAMPLES

Fair Contracts

The formulas for the values of the liability and equity claims presented in the previous section are truly closed formulas that can be readily implemented once the relevant parameters are given.

It is clear that not every choice of parameters will represent fair contracts, i.e., contracts that have been initiated with a fair value split between the stakeholders. For example, the guaranteed interest rate, r_G, and the participation coefficient, δ, cannot both be arbitrarily high (to the benefit of policyholders) with everything else held fixed. So a relevant first question to ask is which combinations of parameters will represent fair contracts. This question can be answered by establishing solutions to the equation

$$L_0 \equiv \alpha A_0 = V_L(A_0,0;\alpha,\delta,\lambda,\sigma,T,r,r_G), \tag{13}$$

which formalizes the requirement that in equilibrium one must establish equality between the liability holders' initial contribution to the total assets and the initial market value of their acquired contingent claim. Since one must have

$$A_0 = V_L(A_0,0) + V_E(A_0,0), \tag{14}$$

an equivalent approach would be to take the equity holders' point of view and explore solutions to

$$E_0 \equiv (1 - \alpha)A_0 = V_E(A_0,0;\alpha,\delta,\lambda,\sigma,T,r,r_G). \tag{15}$$

Whether working with Equation (13) or (15), one must establish solutions via numerical search routines in much the same way as implied volatilities are usually backed out from the Black-Scholes formula. Note, however, that due to the composite and more complex structure of the valuation formulas herein, a full-blown investigation of, e.g., the form of the solution set, comparative statics, conditions for existence and uniqueness of solutions, and so on, will be a formidable task. Thus the article provides some selected representative plots to illustrate some typical relations between parameters of initially fair contracts.

Figures 5 through 7 illustrate the relation between fair values of the participation coefficient, δ, and the guaranteed interest rate, r_G, for some fixed and representative values of the remaining parameters. It is first noted that all these graphs are negatively sloped, as a higher participation coefficient must necessarily be associated with a lower guaranteed interest rate for the contract to be fair to both sides (note in particular that the wealth distribution coefficient, α, is held fixed at 0.80 in these examples).

FIGURE 5

Fair Contracts, Relation Between δ and r_G

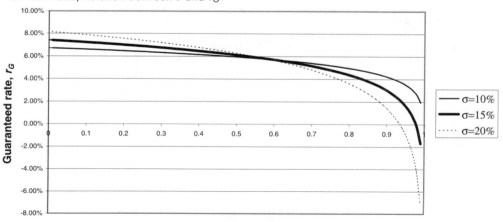

$$\alpha = 0.80, \ r = 6\%, \ T = 20, \ \lambda = 0.80$$

Looking at Figure 5, for high values of the participation coefficient, i.e., for values above approximately 0.6, where the bonus option element dominates the liability holders' contract, a decrease in volatility, σ, would require a higher guaranteed rate if the value split is to remain unaffected. When δ is low and the conditional fixed payment element and the rebate element dominate, this relationship is reversed. Note also that at the point where the three curves intersect, the fair contracts are approximately volatility-neutral in the sense that the effects on the various contract elements of changing the volatility almost exactly offset each other. This feature of the contracts studied is similar to a phenomenon that corporate financial economists refer to as *The Case for Convertibles*. The close relation between the contract studied here and convertible securities has been mentioned. Brennan and Schwartz (1993) offered one of the first satisfactory explanations for the use of convertibles in corporate financing by referring to the relative insensitivity of their value to the risk of the issuing company. Due to the similarity in design, this property is shared by the insurance contracts described in this article. The possibility to obtain risk-insensitive liabilities by appropriate design of contracts is a separate point that insurers may find interesting to explore further.

The graph in Figure 6 is very similar to that in Figure 5 except that the three curves represent different values of time to maturity, T. Again, there seems to be a small set of values of r_G and δ for which the value of the liability holders' contract is insensitive with respect to changes in the time to maturity.

Figure 7 is a typical picture of the effect of changes to the boundary level parameter, λ, on the set of fair combinations of δ and r_G. Note that a higher value of λ benefits the liability holders (provides better security against losses) and hence requires r_G and/or δ to be lowered for the contract to remain fair. Although it is not immediately obvious that a higher λ always works to the benefit of liability holders regardless of the values

FIGURE 6

Fair Contracts, Relation Between δ and r_G

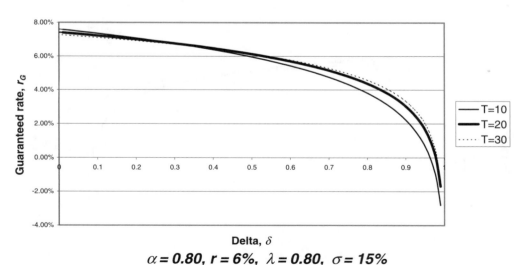

$\alpha = 0.80$, $r = 6\%$, $\lambda = 0.80$, $\sigma = 15\%$

FIGURE 7

Fair Contracts, Relation Between δ and r_G

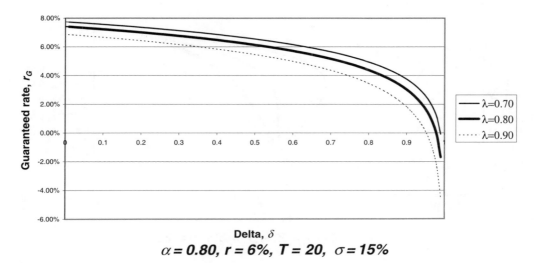

$$\alpha = 0.80, \; r = 6\%, \; T = 20, \; \sigma = 15\%$$

FIGURE 8

Fair Contracts, Relation Between δ and α

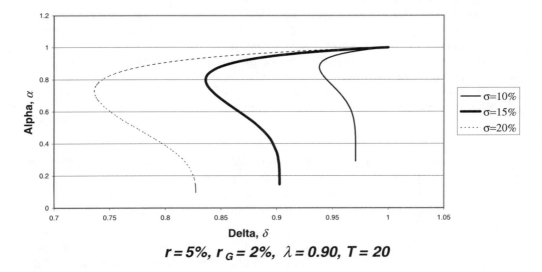

$$r = 5\%, \; r_G = 2\%, \; \lambda = 0.90, \; T = 20$$

of the other parameters, the authors have not been able to generate plots that did not look similar to those in Figure 7.

Figures 8 and 9 show plots of various combinations of the participation coefficient, δ, and the wealth distribution coefficient, α, which represent fair contracts for the other parameters given and for different values of the volatility coefficient (Figure 8) and for different values of the boundary level parameter, λ (Figure 9).The following observations can be made from these figures. First, note that increasing the partici-

FIGURE 9
Fair Contracts, Relation Between δ and α

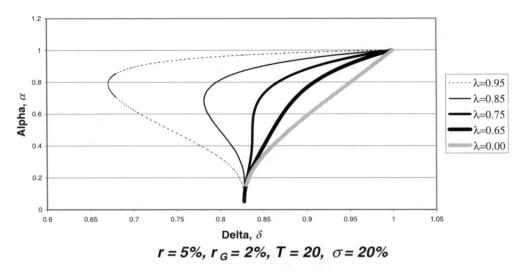

$$r = 5\%, \; r_G = 2\%, \; T = 20, \; \sigma = 20\%$$

pation coefficient toward its maximum value of 1 will force the wealth distribution coefficient, α, toward the value of 1 as well. This means that in the limit where liability holders receive the entire surplus, they will also find themselves as the sole group of stakeholders; i.e., no investors demanding fairness will provide equity for such a "company." Second, for any given σ or λ, a lower boundary to the participation coefficient exists that can be offered in a fair contract. In Figure 8, for example, with $\sigma = 15$ percent, no contract with δ lower than approximately 0.836 can be fair to the liability holders. When volatility is increased this bound is generally lowered. With volatility set at 20 percent, for example, fair contracts exist with δ as low as 0.736. Third, for some, but not all, values of δ two distinct values of α exist that, in conjunction with the other parameters, each represent a fair contract.

Value Components of Fair Contracts

In the analytical part of the article, value formulas were derived for each of the components that make up the various contracts. These separate values did not emerge from the figures discussed above, but Table 2 shows some examples of how the total contract value at the time of negotiation decomposes into the separate elements.

In the table, the total initial assets, A_0, are set at 100 and $\alpha = 0.8$, implying that the sum of the liability contract elements should equal 80 and that the sum of the values of the equity holders' claim elements should equal 20. The risk-free interest rate and the guaranteed rate are fixed at 5 percent and 2 percent, respectively. Time to maturity, T, is 20 years. Each panel of the table represents a different value of λ from the set {0.0,0.8,0.9,1.0,1.1,1.2,1.25}, which includes the minimum and maximum values of λ. Within each panel, volatility varies between 10 and 25 percent, and the participation coefficient, δ, has been numerically determined as the value that makes the contract fair; i.e., V_L is computed to equal 80.

From the table, several interesting observations can be made. For example:

- If volatility is increased, δ must be lowered to maintain a fair value distribution.

- A larger volatility tends to increase the value of the rebate element and to decrease the value of the conditional fixed payment. This is, of course, explained by the fact that generally a larger volatility is associated with a larger probability of an early "barrier hit."

- The larger the λ, the smaller the value of the shorted put option element of the liability holder's contract, and when $\lambda \geq 1$ this element disappears entirely. Remember that the idea of introducing the regulatory boundary was precisely to reduce the value of this element.

- As expected, the value of the equity rebate element is nil when $\lambda \leq 1$ and positive when $\lambda > 1$. When $\lambda \downarrow 0$ (the Briys-Varenne special case), the value of the rebate to liability holders is zero. In the other extreme case where $\lambda = \frac{1}{\alpha} = 1.25$ (last row of Table 2), the contracts cannot really be initiated because A_0 "sits" on the boundary and the initial investment is immediately paid out as a rebate.

The authors leave it to the reader to study the further details of the table.

State-Dependent Intermediate Contract Values

The previous analyses of this section were all centered on constructing and valuing fair contracts at the date of inception, i.e., at time zero. An important property of the model herein is that it can identify fair contracts for a given set of initial conditions. However, equally important, the model can price contracts and their constituting elements at any given point in time given the initially specified terms and conditions, and given information about the present state of the world. This model property makes it a potentially useful tool in relation to the increasing popularity of market value–based accounting in the life insurance and pension business. Properly applied, the model can simply deliver the market values required for market value reporting in the accounting statements and on the balance sheets. At this point, one must emphasize that an informative mark-to-market reporting of the value of the liabilities would require that the option to default is separately disclosed in the balance sheet or in the notes to the accounts. This would provide investors, policyholders, and regulators with one item representing the value of the promises, undiminished by the default probability of the insurer, and a second item representing the value of the put option to default. Suppose, conversely, that the option to default is not unbundled from the other components of an insurance contract. Then mark-to-market of the liabilities would reduce their value (preserving economic surplus) when an insurer approaches insolvency. In turn, this would wrongly suggest the insurer to be in better financial health than when the insurer must report the value of liabilities on a gross basis that is not reduced by the prospects of insolvency.[20] It follows that the estimated value of the put option to default should be a figure of particular interest to regulatory authorities.

In relation to the above discussion and as the final numerical examples herein, see the following cartoon of plots of the values of the liability holders' contract components as a function of the state variable, A_t, at different times during the life of the contract

---

[20] The authors are grateful to Professor David F. Babbel for communicating these insights to us. See also Babbel (1999).

TABLE 2

Decompositions of Contract Values ($A_0 = 100, r = 5\%, r_G = 2\%, \alpha = 0.80, T = 20$)

σ	δ	BO	SP	CFP	RL	$V_L(A_0,0)$	RC	SBO	RE	$V_E(A_0,0)$
					$\lambda = 0.00$					
0.10	0.981	36.47	−0.37	43.90	0.00	80.00	56.47	−36.47	0.00	20.00
0.15	0.959	38.37	−2.27	43.90	0.00	80.00	58.37	−38.37	0.00	20.00
0.20	0.951	41.49	−5.39	43.90	0.00	80.00	61.49	−41.49	0.00	20.00
0.25	0.951	45.20	−9.10	43.90	0.00	80.00	65.20	−45.20	0.00	20.00
					$\lambda = 0.80$					
0.10	0.970	35.81	−0.04	40.57	3.66	80.00	55.81	−35.81	0.00	20.00
0.15	0.902	33.74	−0.05	29.51	16.80	80.00	53.74	−33.74	0.00	20.00
0.20	0.836	30.91	−0.03	19.84	29.28	80.00	50.91	−30.91	0.00	20.00
0.25	0.785	28.36	−0.02	13.35	38.31	80.00	48.36	−28.36	0.00	20.00
					$\lambda = 0.90$					
0.10	0.945	33.95	0.00	36.99	9.07	80.00	53.95	−33.95	0.00	20.00
0.15	0.836	28.58	0.00	24.05	27.37	80.00	48.58	−28.58	0.00	20.00
0.20	0.743	23.87	0.00	15.23	40.90	80.00	43.87	−23.87	0.00	20.00
0.25	0.672	20.42	0.00	9.93	49.66	80.00	40.42	−20.42	0.00	20.00
					$\lambda = 1.00$					
0.10	0.878	29.03	0.00	31.05	19.92	80.00	49.03	−29.03	0.00	20.00
0.15	0.707	20.24	0.00	17.88	41.88	80.00	40.24	−20.24	0.00	20.00
0.20	0.569	14.50	0.00	10.71	54.79	80.00	34.50	−14.50	0.00	20.00
0.25	0.465	10.84	0.00	6.78	62.38	80.00	30.84	−10.84	0.00	20.00
					$\lambda = 1.10$					
0.10	0.833	21.75	0.00	21.91	36.34	80.00	38.12	−21.75	3.63	20.00
0.15	0.668	13.43	0.00	11.11	55.46	80.00	27.88	−13.43	5.55	20.00
0.20	0.540	9.10	0.00	6.31	64.58	80.00	22.64	−9.10	6.46	20.00
0.25	0.442	6.61	0.00	3.90	69.50	80.00	19.66	−6.61	6.95	20.00
					$\lambda=1.20$					
0.10	0.786	9.13	0.00	8.58	62.29	80.00	16.67	−9.13	12.46	20.00
0.15	0.634	4.93	0.00	3.82	71.25	80.00	10.68	−4.93	14.25	20.00
0.20	0.514	3.16	0.00	2.07	74.77	80.00	8.21	−3.16	14.95	20.00
0.25	0.422	2.23	0.00	1.24	76.52	80.00	6.93	−2.23	15.30	20.00
					$\lambda = 1.25$					
all	all	0.00	0.00	0.00	80.00	80.00	0.00	0.00	20.00	20.00

BO: bonus option, SP: shorted put option, CFP: conditional fixed payment, RL: rebate to liability holders, RC: residual call, SBO: shorted bonus option, RE: rebate to equity holders.

FIGURE 10a

Liability Value Components as Function of Total Asset Value $t = 0$

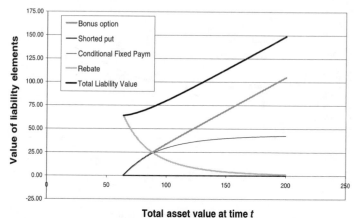

Total asset value at time t

$A_0 = 100, \ \alpha = 0.8, r = 5\%, r_G = 2\%, \ \sigma = 15\%, \ \delta = 0.9015, \ \lambda = 0.8, T = 20$

FIGURE 10b

Liability Value Components as Function of Total Asset Value $t = 10$

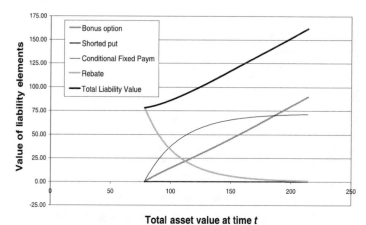

Total asset value at time t

$A_0 = 100, \ \alpha = 0.8, r = 5\%, r_G = 2\%, \ \sigma = 15\%, \ \delta = 0.9015, \ \lambda = 0.8, T = 20$

(Figures 10a–10d). The contract parameters have been set so that the contract was fair at $t = 0$ and the contract element values are plotted for $t = 0+$ (right after inception), $t = 10$, $t = 19.75$, and $t = T = 20$ (the maturity date).

Note in particular that the plots start out not from a zero value of A_t but from the boundary value at time t, and that this lower point of the asset value moves upward as time passes in accordance with the imposed exponential boundary. Note also how the graphs depicting the total liability value tend toward the sharply kinked maturity

FIGURE 10c

Liability Value Components as Function of Total Asset Value $t = 19.75$

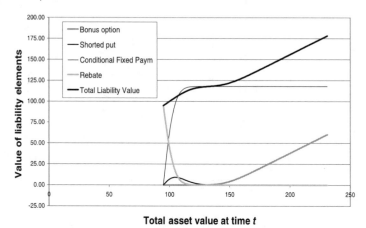

Total asset value at time t

$A_0 = 100, \ \alpha = 0.8, r = 5\%, r_G = 2\%, \ \sigma = 15\%, \ \delta = 0.9015, \ \lambda = 0.8, T = 20$

FIGURE 10d

Liability Value Components as Function of Total Asset Value $t = 20$

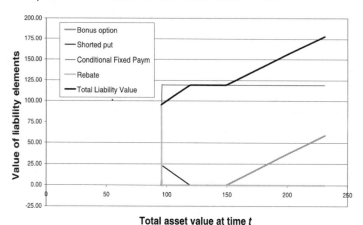

Total asset value at time t

$A_0 = 100, \ \alpha = 0.8, r = 5\%, r_G = 2\%, \ \sigma = 15\%, \ \delta = 0.9015, \ \lambda = 0.8, T = 20$

payoff diagram that is shown in Figure 2.[21] Furthermore, the conditional fixed payment part of the contract increases in value as A_t increases and makes a premature rebate payment less likely. For the same reason, the value of the rebate decreases in A_t. The put option value is negligible unless A_t is in the narrow window between λL_T^G and L_T^G (for $\lambda < 1$), and t is close to T.

---

[21] Here the value of the liability holders' contract is uniformly increasing in A_t, but it is not difficult to construct contracts with a negative gamma when A_t is close to the boundary. This happens because a small movement away from the boundary can actually work to the disadvantage of the policyholders by making a premature rebate payment less likely and since the positive effects of a more likely fixed maturity payment and perhaps more bonus are insufficient to make up for this "loss."

Similar plots of the model's state-dependent market valuation of the equity can be constructed but are omitted here for space considerations.

CONCLUSIONS

This article develops a model in which life insurance liabilities and equity are treated as composite contingent claims with various embedded option features. The equity holders' contract is modeled as a residual claim on total assets reflecting the limited liability of this group of claimants. The liability holders' contract is carefully modeled to reflect some key properties of real-life participating contracts: the guaranteed interest rate, which must at least be credited each period, the right to receive a fair share of any investment surplus (i.e., *participation* as dictated by the contribution principle), and first claim on company assets in the event of default.

Moreover, the authors have assumed the existence of a regulatory authority that monitors the mutually formed company continuously and that has the power to shut down the company if a certain solvency requirement is not met. In this case, recovered assets are distributed prematurely to the stakeholders. The regulatory mechanism introduces a true dynamic element to the model, but it also complicates matters considerably by inducing barrier features into the contracts' embedded option elements. However, closed valuation formulas for the two contract types and their constituting elements can be established.

The article discusses how these valuation formulas are useful from at least two perspectives. First, they can be implemented to determine the set of parameters that characterizes initially fair contracts in the sense that the model's valuation of the contingent contract corresponds to the initial premium. Second, the model can be used for fair market valuation of the equity and liability entries of the company's balance sheet *after* the inception of the contracts, following changes in market conditions (state variables). This form of application is in line with recent initiatives by the accounting profession (FASB, IASC), which seems to continue the process of strengthening its recommendations in favor of market value accounting.

Some of the model properties were explored and discussed via representative numerical examples. For example, comparing the results of the model herein with those of the "static" model of Briys and de Varenne (1997), one saw that a regulatory intervention boundary can place an effective restriction on the value of the limited liability put option. This observation indicates that the companies' potential moral hazard problem, which is created by the incentives to change the risk characteristics of its assets in order to cause a transfer of wealth from policyholders to equity holders, is overestimated in the static model.

Some natural paths for further research emerge. Already mentioned is the fact that many insurers now face claims from distinct groups of liability holders distinguished by different guaranteed interest rates in their policies. This raises the problem of how to avoid inequitable treatment of different classes of policyholders within the same fund. Some companies, like JØP in Denmark, have had tremendous concerns over the definition of a correct and fair distribution policy when the situation of the asset side does not permit the application of an identical surplus distribution policy across all policyholders.[22] The model presented here could be extended to include more than one homogeneous class of policyholders. This could guide these companies to a more correct policy based on market value considerations. It would also be straightforward to incorporate mortality risk into the model along the lines of Jensen et al. (2001).

Another possible extension of this model would be to incorporate a third stakeholder in the form of an external guarantor of the liability holders' deposits. Such a scheme could be fair to all sides if the guarantor is compensated for the issued guarantee in the form of a contingent payoff (rebate) out of recovered assets if the company is closed.

Finally, the cost of a default-triggered put option as the one issued by a guarantor is significantly reduced if introducing a regulatory boundary, as suggested herein. Hence, it would be natural to let the jobs as solvency monitor and default guarantor go hand in hand. A small digression from this research direction could be to restrict monitoring events (audits) to a discrete set of dates.

Appendix

Proof of Theorem 1: Recall first that one has (from Equation (10))

$$A_s = A_t \cdot e^{(r-\frac{1}{2}\sigma^2)(s-t)+\sigma(W_s^Q-W_t^Q)}, \quad s \in [t,T], \tag{A1}$$

and the exponential knockout barrier

$$B_s = B_t \cdot e^{r_G(s-t)} = \lambda L_t \cdot e^{r_G(s-t)}, \quad s \in [t,T]. \tag{A2}$$

Assuming $A_t > B_t$ (the barrier is approached from above), the first-hitting time τ is given as

$$
\begin{aligned}
\tau &= \inf\{s > t | A_s \le B_s\} \\
&= \inf\left\{s > t | A_t \cdot e^{(r-r_G-\frac{1}{2}\sigma^2)(s-t)+\sigma(W_s^Q-W_t^Q)} \le B_t \equiv \lambda L_t^G\right\}.
\end{aligned}
\tag{A3}
$$

Now turn to the specific parts of Theorem 1.

Part (i). Rewriting the relevant expectation, one gets

$$
\begin{aligned}
& e^{-r(T-t)}E_t^Q\{\delta[\alpha A_T - L_T^G]^+ \cdot 1_{\{\tau>T\}}\} \\
&= \delta\alpha e^{-r(T-t)}E_t^Q\left\{\left[A_T - \frac{L_T^G}{\alpha}\right]^+ \cdot 1_{\{\tau>T\}}\right\} \\
&= \delta\alpha e^{-(r-r_G)(T-t)}E_t^Q\left\{\left[A_t \cdot e^{(r-r_G-\frac{1}{2}\sigma^2)(T-t)+\sigma(W_T^Q-W_t^Q)} - \frac{L_T^G}{\alpha}\right]^+ \cdot 1_{\{\tau>T\}}\right\}. \tag{A4}
\end{aligned}
$$

---

[22] JØP (Juristernes og Økonomernes Pensionskasse) is the pension fund of all Danish individuals with university degrees in economics or law!

With relation (A3) in mind, recognize this expression as $\delta\alpha$ times the time t value of a standard knockout call option with maturity date T, "interest rate" $r - r_G$, exercise price L_t^G/α, and constant knockout barrier at $B_t = \lambda L_t^G$. The solution to this problem is known—see, e.g., Björk (1998) or Hull (2000)—so by performing the necessary substitutions, the desired result obtains.

Part (ii). First,

$$e^{-r(T-t)}E_t^Q\left\{L_T^G \cdot 1_{\{\tau>T\}}\right\} = L_T^G \cdot e^{-r(T-t)}Q(\tau > T), \tag{A5}$$

so the risk-neutral "survival probability" (no absorption before time T) must be established in relation to the problem described earlier in this proof. Denoting the first-hitting time density in relation to Equation (A3) as $g(\cdot)$, establish the result by straightforward integration, i.e.,

$$Q(\tau > T) = 1 - \int_t^T g(u)du. \tag{A6}$$

The first-hitting time density, $g(\cdot)$, can be found in Ingersoll (1987).

Part (iii). Via manipulations similar to those in the proof of part (i), the value of the shorted put option element is $-1_{\{\lambda<1\}}$ times the time t value of a knockout put option with maturity date T, "interest rate" $r - r_G$, exercise price L_t^G, and constant knockout barrier at $B_t = \lambda L_t^G$. The solution to this problem is known (see, e.g., Hull, 2000), and the result herein obtains following the necessary substitutions.

Part (iv). To establish this result, first write

$$E_t^Q\left\{e^{-r(\tau-t)}(\lambda \wedge 1)L_0 e^{r_G\tau}\right\} = (\lambda \wedge 1)L_t^G E_t^Q\left\{e^{-(r-r_G)(\tau-t)}\right\}$$

$$= (\lambda \wedge 1)L_t^G \int_t^T e^{-(r-r_G)(u-t)} \cdot g(u)du, \tag{A7}$$

and then perform the integration directly using the well-known hitting time density referred to in the proof of part (ii). The authors finally remind the reader that a detailed proof is available from the authors on request. ∎

REFERENCES

Babbel, D. F., 1994, A Perspective on Investment Laws for Insurers, *Chartered Life Underwriter Journal*, September: 72-77.

Babbel, D. F., 1999, Components of Insurance Firm Value and the Present Value of Liabilities, in: D. F. Babbel and F. Fabozzi, eds., *Insurance Company Investment Management* (New Hope, PA: Frank J. Fabozzi Associates).

Babbel, D. F., and C. Merrill, 1998, Economic Valuation Models for Insurers, *North American Actuarial Journal*, 2(3): 1-17.

Babbel, D. F., and C. Merrill 1999, Toward a Unified Valuation Model for Life Insurers, in: J. D. Cummins and A. M. Santomero, eds., *Changes in the Life Insurance Industry: Efficiency, Technology and Risk Management* (Norwell, MA: Kluwer).

Baccinello, A. R., and F. Ortu, 1993a, Pricing Equity-Linked Life Insurance With Endogenous Minimum Guarantees: A Corrigendum, *Insurance: Mathematics and Economics*, 13: 303-304.

Baccinello, A. R., and F. Ortu, 1993b, Pricing Equity-Linked Life Insurance With Endogenous Minimum Guarantees, *Insurance: Mathematics and Economics*, 12(3): 245-258.

Björk, T., 1998, *Arbitrage Theory in Continuous Time* (New York: Oxford University Press).

Black, F., and M. Scholes, 1973, The Pricing of Options and Corporate Liabilities, *Journal of Political Economy*, 81(3): 637-654.

Black, F., and H. D. Skipper, 1994, *Life Insurance*, 12th ed. (Englewood Cliffs, N.J.: Prentice Hall).

Boyle, P. P., and M. R. Hardy, 1997, Reserving for Maturity Guarantees: Two Approaches, *Insurance: Mathematics and Economics*, 21(3): 113-127.

Boyle, P. P., and E. S. Schwartz, 1977, Equilibrium Prices of Guarantees Under Equity-Linked Contracts, *Journal of Risk and Insurance*, 44: 639-660.

Brennan, M. J., 1993, Aspects of Insurance, Intermediation and Finance, *The Geneva Papers on Risk and Insurance Theory*, 18(1): 7-30.

Brennan, M. J., and E. S. Schwartz, 1976, The Pricing of Equity-Linked Life Insurance Policies With an Asset Value Guarantee, *Journal of Financial Economics*, 3: 195-213.

Brennan, M. J., and E. S. Schwartz, 1979, Alternative Investment Strategies for the Issuers of Equity-Linked Life Insurance Policies With an Asset Value Guarantee, *Journal of Business*, 52(1): 63-93.

Brennan, M. J., and E. S. Schwartz, 1993, The Case for Convertibles, in: D. H. Chew, ed., *The New Corporate Finance: Where Theory Meets Practice*. McGraw-Hill Series in Advanced Topics in Finance and Accounting, 288-297.

Briys, E., and F. de Varenne, 1994, Life Insurance in a Contingent Claim Framework: Pricing and Regulatory Implications, *The Geneva Papers on Risk and Insurance Theory*, 19(1): 53-72.

Briys, E., and F. de Varenne, 1997, On the Risk of Life Insurance Liabilities: Debunking Some Common Pitfalls, *Journal of Risk and Insurance*, 64(4): 673-694.

Forfar, D. O., and N. B. Masters, 1999, Developing an International Accounting Standard for Life Insurance Business, Paper presented to the Faculty of Actuaries, March 15.

Grosen, A., and P. L. Jørgensen, 1997, Valuation of Early Exercisable Interest Rate Guarantees, *Journal of Risk and Insurance*, 64(3): 481-503.

Grosen, A., and P. L. Jørgensen, 2000, Fair Valuation of Life Insurance Liabilities: The Impact of Interest Rate Guarantees, Surrender Options, and Bonus Policies, *Insurance: Mathematics and Economics*, 26(1): 37-57.

Han, L.-M., G. C. Lai, and R. C. Witt, 1997, A Financial-Economic Evaluation of Insurance Guaranty Fund System: An Agency Cost Perspective, *Journal of Banking and Finance*, 21(8): 1107-1129.

Harrison, M. J., and D. M. Kreps, 1979, Martingales and Arbitrage in Multiperiod Securities Markets, *Journal of Economic Theory*, 20: 381-408.

Hull, J. C., 2000, *Options, Futures, and Other Derivatives*, 4th ed., (Upper Saddle River, N.J.: Prentice-Hall, Inc).

Ingersoll, J. E., Jr., 1987, *Theory of Financial Decision Making* (Totowa, N.J.: Rowan & Littlefield Publishers, Inc.).

Jensen, B., P. L. Jørgensen, and A. Grosen, 2001, A Finite Difference Approach to the Valuation of Path-Dependent Life Insurance Liabilities, *The Geneva Papers on Risk and Insurance Theory*, 26(1): 57-84.

Kalra, R., and G. Jain, 1997, A Continuous-Time Model to Determine the Intervention Policy for PBGC, *Journal of Banking and Finance*, 21: 1159-1177.

Merton, R. C., 1974, On the Pricing of Corporate Debt: The Risk Structure of Interest Rates, *The Journal of Finance*, 29: 449-470.

Merton, R. C., 1977, An Analytic Derivation of the Cost of Deposit Insurance and Loan Guarantees: An Application of Modern Option Pricing Theory, *Journal of Banking and Finance*, 1: 3-11.

Merton, R. C., 1978, On the Cost of Deposit Insurance When There Are Surveillance Costs, *Journal of Business*, 51: 439-452.

Merton, R. C., 1989, On the Application of the Continuous-Time Theory of Finance to Financial Intermediation and Insurance, *The Geneva Papers on Risk and Insurance Theory*, 14: 225-262.

Merton, R. C., 1990, *Continuous-Time Finance* (Padstow, Great Britain: Basil Blackwell Inc.).

Merton, R. C., and Z. Bodie, 1992, On the Management of Financial Guarantees, *Financial Management*, Winter: 87-109.

Miltersen, K. R., and S.-A. Persson, 1998, Guaranteed Investment Contracts: Distributed and Undistributed Excess Return, Working paper (Odense University).

Nielsen, J. A., and K. Sandmann, 1995, Equity-Linked Life Insurance: A Model With Stochastic Interest Rates, *Insurance: Mathematics and Economics*, 16: 225-253.

Smith, M. L., 1982, The Life Insurance Policy as an Options Package, *Journal of Risk and Insurance*, 49(4): 583-601.

Vanderhoof, I. T., and E. I. Altman, eds., 1998, *The Fair Value of Insurance Liabilities*, Kluwer Academic Publishers, The New York University Salomon Center Series on Financial Markets and Institutions.

Recent Court Decisions

Jeffrey W. Stempel
University of Nevada–Las Vegas

Supreme Court Holds That State Statute Providing for Revocation of Former Spouse as Life Insurance Beneficiary Is Preempted by ERISA

Egelhoff v. Egelhoff, 532 U.S. 141, 121 S.Ct. 1322, 149 L.Ed. 2d 264 (U.S. Supreme Court—March 21, 2001)

A State of Washington statute provides that the designation of a spouse as the beneficiary of a nonprobate asset is automatically revoked by operation of law upon divorce. The statute and its applicability to life insurance provided by an employee benefits plan subject to ERISA (the Employee Retirement Income Security Act) became the subject of the U.S. Supreme Court's latest foray into the field of ERISA preemption. The Court found that the state statute preempted under the circumstances of the case, notwithstanding that distribution of marital assets is a traditional state function not ordinarily regulated by the federal government.

Donna Rae and David Egelhoff were once married. David was an employee of Boeing, the large aircraft manufacturer, which provided him with both a life insurance policy and a pension plan. Because these were employer-provided benefits plans, they were governed by ERISA. In April 1994, the Egelhoffs divorced. David was in a car accident two months later and died within months, creating the dispute that led to this decision.

At the time of David's death, Donna Rae continued to be the listed beneficiary under both the life insurance policy and the pension plan. The life insurer paid her benefits of $56,000. David's children from a prior marriage (and his heirs under the state intestacy statute) sued Donna Rae in Washington state court seeking to recover the life insurance proceeds. They based their claim on Wash. Rev. Code §11.07.010(2)(a)(1994), which provides:

> If a marriage is dissolved or invalidated, a provision made prior to that event that relates to the payment or transfer at death of the decedent's interest in a nonprobate asset in favor of or granting an interest or power to the decedent's former spouse is revoked. A provision affected by this section must be interpreted, and the nonprobate assets affected passes, as if the former spouse failed to survive the decedent, having died at the time of entry of the decree of dissolution or declaration of invalidity.

The statute defines "nonprobate assets" to include life insurance policies and pension benefits.

In other words, former spouses cease being beneficiaries for these types of assets to protect against a former spouse unwittingly leaving this property to an ex-spouse simply because of a failure to remember to change the beneficiary. If an ex-spouse wishes to leave this sort of property to the other ex-spouse, the statute is designed to force a new beneficiary designation so that property is not unwittingly given to a former spouse who is now the object of enmity rather than affection. Similarly, as one might intuit from the suit of the Egelhoff children, the statute seeks to reduce the possibility that a former spouse will receive funds that the decedent ex-spouse might well have preferred go to his or her children.

The Washington courts, including the state supreme court, found for the Egelhoff children and against Donna Rae, who had raised a defense of ERISA preemption to the suit, arguing that the state law could not govern the federally regulated Boeing employee benefits plan. ERISA provides in part that any state law "relating to" a covered benefits plan is preempted. The Washington Supreme Court found no preemption, holding that the statute was not sufficiently connected to the ERISA plan and that the statute did not substantially interfere with the operation of ERISA plans to warrant preemption. *See In re Estate of Egelhoff*, 93 Wash. 2d 557, 989 P.2d 80 (1999). Courts had divided over the issue, prompting the U.S. Supreme Court to consider the issue. *Compare Emard v. Hughes Aircraft Co.*, 153 F.3d 949 (9th Cir. 1998) (finding, like Washington Supreme Court, that there is no ERISA preemption) *with Manning v. Hayes*, 212 F.3d 866 (5th Cir. 2000) (finding preemption); *Metropolitan Life Ins. Co. v. Hanslip*, 939 F.2d 904 (10th Cir. 1991) (same).

The U.S. Supreme Court reversed, finding the state statute preempted. The statute binds ERISA plan administrators to a particular choice of rules for determining beneficiary status.

* * *

One of the principal goals of ERISA is to enable employers "to establish a uniform administrative scheme, which provides a set of standard procedures to guide processing of claims and disbursement of benefits." Uniformity is impossible, however, if plans are subject to different legal obligations in different states.

> The Washington statute at issue here poses precisely that threat. Plan administrators cannot make payments simply by identifying the beneficiary specified by the plan documents. Instead, they must familiarize themselves with state statutes so that they can determine whether the named beneficiary's status has been "revoked" by operation of law. And in this context the burden is exacerbated by the choice-of-law problems that may confront an administrator when the employer is located in one state, the plan participant lives in another, and the participant's former spouse lives in a third. In such a situation, administrators might find that plan payments are subject to conflicting legal obligations.

121 S.Ct. at 1327-28 (citations omitted).

The Court was unmoved that the Washington statute protects plan administrators from liability for erroneous payment of benefits to a former spouse unless the administrator had "actual knowledge" of the divorce or other invalidation of the marriage. *Id.* at *15. The Court was, however, concerned with one of the Egelhoff children's arguments that, if ERISA preempted the revocation of ex-spouse as beneficiary statute, ERISA must also preempt other state laws such as those that prevent a beneficiary from collecting benefits after murdering a testator or insurance holder. The Court dodged the issue but suggested it would draw a line separating the Washington law from the "slayer" statutes if necessary in a subsequent case.

> In the ERISA context, these slayer statutes could revoke the beneficiary status of someone who murdered a plan participant. Those statutes are not before us, so we do not decide the issue. We note, however, that the principle underlying the statutes—which have been adopted by nearly every state—is well established in the law and has a long historical pedigree predating ERISA. *See, e.g., Riggs v. Palmer,* 115 N.Y. 506, 22 N.E. 188 (1889) (the famous New York case that refused to award benefits under a will as written where the beneficiary had murdered the maker of the will). And because the statutes are more or less uniform nationwide, their interference with the aims of ERISA is at least debatable.

121 S.Ct. at 1330.

Justices Scalia and Ginsburg concurred in the result, primarily to reiterate the view they have expressed in earlier cases that ERISA preemption should be decided according to ordinary preemption principles rather than solely by focus on the "relate to" language of ERISA's preemption provision. 121 S.Ct. at 1330-31.

Justices Breyer and Stevens dissented, arguing that the Washington statute did not interfere with the Boeing plan (or ERISA, for that matter) in a sufficiently significant way to warrant preemption. 121 S.Ct. at 1331. According to the dissenters, David Egelhoff's Boeing plan did not specifically address the issue of whether the decedent employee's benefits should go to the former spouse or to the former spouse's heirs-at-law. Therefore, argued Justice Breyer, it should not violate ERISA for state law to provide an answer to the question. The dissent emphasized the degree to which family property division was historically a matter regulated by the states and expressed concern that the Court was federalizing this area of the law when Congress had not intended such a result. The dissent was also concerned about the equities of the case.

> In forbidding Washington to apply that assumption (of revoking the ex-spouse's designation as beneficiary) here, the Court permits a divorced wife, who *already* acquired, during the divorce proceeding, her fair share of the couple's community property, to receive in addition the benefits that the divorce court awarded to her former husband. To be more specific, Donna Egelhoff already received a business, an IRA account, and stock; David received, among other things, 100% of his pension benefits. David did not change the beneficiary designation in the pension plan or life insurance plan during the six-month period between his divorce and his death. As a result, Donna will now receive a windfall of approximately $80,000 at the

expense of David's children. The State of Washington enacted a statute to prevent precisely this kind of unfair result. But the Court, relying on an inconsequential administrative burden, concluded that Congress required it.

121 S. Ct. at 1334 (emphasis in original, citations omitted).

The dissenters also argued that the *Egelhoff* holding was in tension with the Court's other ERISA preemption cases of recent vintage.

U.S. SUPREME COURT RULES ARBITRATION AGREEMENT NOT DEFECTIVE MERELY BECAUSE IT FAILS TO SPECIFY RELATIVE RESPONSIBILITIES OF THE PARTIES FOR PAYING COST OF ARBITRATION

Green Tree Financial Corporation–Alabama v. Randolph, 531 U.S. 79, 121 S.Ct. 513, 148 L.Ed. 2d 373 (U.S. Supreme Court—December 11, 2000)

Larketta Randolph purchased a mobile home in Opelika, Ala., and financed the purchase through Green Tree Financial Corporation's Alabama subsidiary. The sales contract required Randolph to buy "Vendor's Single Interest insurance, which protects the vendor or lienholder against the costs of repossession in the event of default." The agreement also provided that "all disputes arising from, or relating to, the contract, whether arising under case law or statutory law, would be resolved by binding arbitration." 121 S.Ct. at 518.

The agreement was silent on the question of who would pay the costs of the arbitration, such as filing fees and arbitrator's costs, and was similarly silent as to the amounts of those fees. The lower federal appellate court was concerned that substantial arbitration costs could be imposed and thus materially inhibit Randolph's ability to protect her statutory rights. The U.S. Supreme Court found that this silence did not make the agreement unenforceable. "The 'risk' that Randolph will be saddled with prohibitive costs is too speculative [based on the record of the case] to justify the invalidation of the arbitration agreement." 121 S.Ct. at 522.

The Court also concluded that a trial court order directing an arbitration to proceed was a final decision that was then appealable under the appellate doctrines of the federal courts. 121 S.Ct. at 519-21.

MINNESOTA PERMITS HMOS TO SUE TOBACCO COMPANIES WITHOUT NEED TO BE PURCHASER OF PRODUCTS OR TO PROVE RELIANCE ON COMPANY STATEMENTS; HMOS MAY SEEK PAYMENTS FROM TOBACCO COMPANIES FOR AMOUNTS EXPENDED IN HEALTH CARE BASED ON ALLEGED MISREPRESENTATION UNDER STATE SALES LAWS

Group Health Plan, Inc., v. Philip Morris, Inc., et al., 621 N.W.2d 2 (Minnesota Supreme Court—January 11, 2001)

The saga of claims against cigarette manufacturers continues. In the late 1990s, an alliance of state attorneys general brought claims against the major tobacco companies seeking reimbursement for public health funds spent on smoking-related diseases. The result was a multibillion-dollar settlement, including a large award of counsel fees for many of the lawyers who represented states on a contingency fee basis and often advanced their own funds to prosecute the litigation on behalf of the states. Minnesota did not participate in the omnibus settlement but instead went to trial against the tobacco companies and prevailed, arguably obtaining more funds than it would have gained as its share under the almost global state settlement.

But that is only the government-vs.-tobacco part of the story. In the aftermath of that litigation, private health providers such as insurers, health maintenance organizations (HMOs), and Blue Cross–Blue Shield plans have moved to bring similar reimbursement actions against cigarette manufacturers. One such action has been brought by major Minnesota-based HMOs in federal district court. In response to defense objections to the propriety of such claims, the federal court certified two questions for review by the Minnesota Supreme Court.

A "certified" question takes place when a federal court asks the relevant state supreme court to render a pronouncement on a matter of state substantive law so that the federal court may be properly informed of the correct applicable law. Although much federal court litigation involves federal law (the Constitution, U.S. statutes, international treaties, etc.), a good deal of the disputing in federal court is lodged in these courts because the litigants are from different states. But the controlling law is then usually the state law of the state with the closest connection to the controversy. Thus, the U.S. district court asked the Minnesota Supreme Court for guidance on the following two questions:

1. Must a private plaintiff bringing a claim of misrepresentation have been a purchaser of the product to have the right to bring a claim? The question was of course important because the HMOs were not asserting that they used cigarettes and became diseased (try to imagine an HMO with lung cancer). Rather, the HMO claimed that many of its patients smoked, became afflicted with tobacco-related diseases, and required medical care, causing injury to the HMOs.

2. To prevail in a misrepresentation action, must a private plaintiff prove that it relied on inaccurate statements made by the defendant? Again, the HMO entities were of course not arguing that they were lured into smoking by false information or concealment of health hazards. Rather, the HMOs argued that their patients were the victims of industry misrepresentation, became ill, required extra health care, and caused economic damage to the HMOs.

The Minnesota Supreme Court answered both questions in favor of the HMOs suing the tobacco companies. *See* 621 N.W.2d at 2-3 2001 Minn. LEXIS 3 at *2-*3. A medical provider plaintiff, at least in Minnesota, is permitted to sue a product manufacturer without having itself purchased the product or relied upon the manufacturer's statements about the product. "It will be necessary, however, for plaintiffs to prove a causal nexus between the conduct alleged to violate [the statutes] and the damages claimed." 621 N.W.2d at 3.

The claims at issue are based on the state's statutes concerning misrepresentation in the sale of a product. The court relied extensively on the legislative history of the statutes. *See* 621 N.W.2d at 9-10. However, many other states have similar statutes, which suggests that other states addressing the question may well align with Minnesota on the issue. *See, e.g., Van Dyke v. St. Paul Fire & Marine Ins. Co.,* 388 Mass.

671, 448 N.E.2d 357 (Mass. 1983) (Massachusetts Supreme Judicial Court takes similar view of similar statute in case relied upon by Minnesota court in *Group Health* [see 621 N.W.2d at 10-11]).

To some extent, the decision was foreshadowed. The state supreme court had previously found that Blue Cross and Blue Shield of Minnesota was entitled to sue the tobacco companies, making identical claims. *See State by Humphrey v. Philip Morris, Inc.*, 551 N.W.2d 490 (Minn. 1996).

The tobacco defendants attempted to avoid the *Humphrey* precedent by arguing that the term *person* in the relevant statutes logically means consumers and not merchants, such as an HMO. The court rejected this defense, finding that entities injured by a misrepresentation qualified as "persons" entitled to sue if the facts supported the claim. *See* 621 N.W.2d at 9-10.

PENNSYLVANIA SUPREME COURT, AFTER REMAND FROM U.S. SUPREME COURT, REAFFIRMS DECISION THAT ACTIONS AGAINST HMOs FOR NEGLIGENT FAILURE TO AUTHORIZE TREATMENT ARE NOT PREEMPTED BY ERISA, BUT FEDERAL APPEALS COURT SITTING IN PHILADELPHIA REACHES OPPOSITE CONCLUSION IN CASE WITH SIMILAR FACTS

Pappas v. Asbel, 564 Pa. 407, 768 A.2d 1089 (Pennsylvania Supreme Court—April 3, 2001)
Pryzbowski v. U.S. Healthcare, Inc., 245 F.3d 266 (U.S. Court of Appeal, Third Circuit—March 27, 2001).

In a decision reconsidered because of an intervening U.S. Supreme Court decision, the Pennsylvania Supreme Court held that a claim against a health maintenance organization (HMO) for failing to authorize treatment of a patient could be maintained under state law. At 11 a.m. on May 21, 1991, Basil Pappas was admitted to Haverford Community Hospital in the Philadelphia suburbs and diagnosed with an epidural abscess creating pressure on his spinal cord.

The treating physician regarded this as a neurological emergency and recommended that Pappas be immediately transferred to Jefferson University Hospital in Philadelphia. An ambulance arrived at 12:40 p.m. But at that point, U.S. Healthcare, the HMO that insured Pappas, denied authorization for treatment at Jefferson, apparently because it was not a participating hospital in Pappas's U.S. Healthcare plan. The doctor protested and by 1:05 p.m., U.S. Healthcare responded, continuing to deny treatment at Jefferson but to permit transfer of the patient to either Hahnemann or Temple University hospitals. Pappas was eventually taken to Hahnemann by 3:30 p.m. The pressure on his spinal cord caused permanent quadriplegia, prompting Pappas to sue both his primary doctor for medical malpractice and Haverford for inordinate delay in treatment.

Haverford brought U.S. Healthcare into the action with a third-party complaint, alleging that the HMO's refusal to authorize the original planned referral to Jefferson Hospital was a significant part of the delay that in significant part led to the tragedy. U.S. Healthcare raised the defense of ERISA preemption, arguing that it could not be sued under state tort law because Pappas was covered pursuant to an employee benefits plan that was subject to ERISA preemption. U.S. Healthcare argued that ERISA's broad preemption clause stating that any law "relating to" a plan was pre-empted barred the Pappas action.

The Pennsylvania Supreme Court rejected the preemption defense in its first opinion. *See Pappas v. Asbel*, 555 Pa. 342, 724 A.2d 889 (Pa. 1998). U.S. Healthcare, by now part of Aetna, sought review by the U.S. Supreme Court. The High Court remanded the case to Pennsylvania for reconsideration in light of *Pegram v. Herdrich*, 530 U.S. 211, 120 S.Ct. 2143, 147 L.Ed.2d 164 (June 12, 2000). In *Pegram*, the Court held that HMOs making medical treatment decisions or "mixed" decisions regarding coverage and treatment were not "fiduciaries" under ERISA and hence were not subject to the fiduciary liability sections of ERISA. However, the *Pegram* Court did strongly suggest that HMOs acting in this capacity were also outside the protection provided by ERISA's preemption provisions.

Certainly, this was the view of the *Pappas* Court, which reaffirmed its earlier ruling after discussing *Pegram*. *See* 768 A.2d at 415. The *Pappas* Court also reviewed the U.S. Supreme Court's ERISA preemption jurisprudence, which it continued to regard as moving away from the earlier ERISA jurisprudence of extremely broad preemption toward more traditional, restrained notions of preemption. *See* 768 A.2d at 1092-93.

The *Pappas* Court was aware that plaintiff Herdrich in the *Pegram* case has been permitted to pursue a medical malpractice action in Illinois state court, where the claim arose, and that the *Pegram v. Herdrich* facts were analogous to those of *Pappas*. Herdrich was receiving treatment for abdominal pains but was required to wait for treatment and to go to a hospital selected by the HMO. During the interim delay, Herdrich's appendix ruptured. In light of the medical treatment decisions at issue in *Pappas* (and *Pegram* for that matter), the *Pappas* Court rejected the HMO's argument that U.S. Healthcare had made only a coverage determination in refusing to permit the transfer to Jefferson Hospital. *See* 768 A.2d at 1097-98.

In lone dissent, Justice Saylor argued that *Pegram* does not clearly authorize such negligence actions against the HMO even if malpractice actions against the doctor are permitted without ERISA preemption. "Although it has been suggested that the reasoning from *Pegram II* [the U.S. Supreme Court opinion] has effectively overruled the latter line of decisions [finding preemption], reserving ERISA preemption exclusively for the narrow category of claims implicating pure eligibility determination by an HMO unrelated to medical diagnosis and decision-making, the assessment in the aftermath of *Pegram II* has remained mixed." 768 A.2d at 1097-98.

Justice Saylor's statement is correct as far as it goes. However, the majority of scholars have with near uniformity analyzed *Pegram* as overruling precedent that had barred claims against the HMO for decisions impacting medical treatment. *See* Jeffrey W. Stempel and Nadia von Magdenko, *ERISA, HMOs and the Public Interest After* Pegram v. Herdrich, 36 TORT & INS. L.J. 687 (2001); James J. Brudney, *The Changing Complexion of Workplace Law: Labor and Employment Decisions of the Supreme Court's 1999-2000 Term*, 16 LAB. LAW. 151, 195 (2000); Thomas R. McLean, M.D., and Edward P. Richards, *Managed Care Liability for Breach Fiduciary Duty After* Pegram v. Herdrich: *The End of ERISA Preemption for State Law Liability for Medical Care Decision Making*, 53 FLA. L. REV. 1, 19-45 (2001).

On a related front of ERISA preemption and health insurer liability, courts also appear with increasing frequency to be permitting bad faith actions against HMOs providing coverage pursuant to an ERISA plan. In *Pilot Life Ins. Co. v. Dedeaux*, 481 U.S. 41, 107 S.Ct. 1549, 95 L.Ed. 2d 39 (1987), the U.S. Supreme Court found that Louisiana's bad faith cause of action was preempted by ERISA because it "related to" an ERISA plan but was not "specifically directed to the insurance industry." Although bad faith actions against noninsurers are rare in Louisiana, the tort is technically available against other parties.

But where a state's bad faith cause of action is limited to insurance, courts have found *Pilot Life* not to control and that ERISA is not a bar to the action because ERISA specifically saves from preemption state laws regulating insurance. *See, e.g., Gilbert v. Alta Health & Life Ins. Co.*, 122 F. Supp.2d 1267; *Hill v. Blue Cross Blue Shield of Alabama*, 117 F. Supp.2d 1209 (N.D. Ala. 2000); *Lewis v. Aetna U.S. Healthcare*, 78 F. Supp.2d 1202 (N.D. Okla. 1999). But *see Greene v. Well Care HMO, Inc.*, 778 So. 2d 1037 (Fla. App. 4th Dist.—February 14, 2001) (Florida does not permit bad faith cause of action against HMOs, as they are specifically exempted from the relevant section of state insurance code). The decisions permitting bad faith actions against health insurers have been spurred in part and supported by *Unum Life Ins. Co. v. Ward*, 526 U.S. 358, 119 S.Ct. 1380, 143 L.Ed.2d 462 (1999), which held that California's rule that late notice invalidated insurance coverage only if the insurer was prejudiced by the delay was a law regulating insurance within the meaning of ERISA's savings clause.

Reading *Pegram, Pappas*, and the scholarly commentary, one might think that today, an HMO is not immunized by ERISA whenever it is making a decision that in some way affects a patient's medical care—but that is not quite correct, as demonstrated by *Pryzbowski v. U.S. Healthcare, Inc.*, 245 F.3d 266 (3d Cir. 2001).

In *Pryzbowski*, the U.S. Court of Appeals for the Third Circuit (which includes Pennsylvania, New Jersey, Delaware, and the U.S. Virgin Islands) found ERISA to preempt a claim against an HMO arising out of its refusal to agree to let the patient be treated by surgical specialists at an "out-of-network" hospital. The *Pryzbowski* Court regarded this as an administrative decision by the HMO rather than as a mixed question of coverage eligibility and medical treatment.

Pryzbowski began experiencing severe back pains in late 1993 and sought treatment from her regular primary care physician. She had undergone back surgery in the past, which had been covered by her previous health care plan. After investigation, her doctor requested that she consult with the neurosurgeon who had performed a prior surgery. However, this neurosurgeon was not a participant in the U.S. Healthcare plan that currently covered Pryzbowski. U.S. Healthcare approved the consultation, and the neurosurgeon

> concluded that surgery was needed and that the following specialists or specialists' services were required: spinal instrumentation and fusion by a separate orthopedic surgeon, pulmonary clearance and follow-up, consultation with a pain management physician, and a psychological assessment and follow-up. The specialists to whom he referred her were also associated

with Thomas Jefferson University Hospital in Philadelphia and outside the U.S. Healthcare network.

245 F.3d at 269.

U.S. Healthcare refused to approve the recommended treatment of further surgery and treatment by out-of-network doctors. But Pryzbowski did see in-network doctors specializing in pain management and mental health. Pryzbowski continued to seek the recommended out-of-network treatment, which U.S. Healthcare approved on June 30, 1994, approximately seven months after Pryzbowski first came to her doctor. Despite the surgery, she continued to suffer severe back pain. The treating neurosurgeon blamed this on "the significant delay that occurred between the onset of the symptomatology and the surgical intervention." 245 F.3d at 269-70 (quoting neurosurgeon).

Pryzbowski sued her doctors and the HMO, alleging negligent and careless delay in approving urgently needed surgery. U.S. Healthcare argued that the claims against it were preempted by ERISA as essentially "pure" administrative decisions lacking a sufficient component of medical treatment. The Third Circuit agreed.

> Underlying these allegations of delay is the policy adopted by U.S. Healthcare (and many other HMOs) requiring beneficiaries either to use in-network specialists or to obtain approval from the HMO for out-of-network specialists. These activities fall within the realm of the administration of benefits.

245 F.3d at 274.

In essence, the *Pryzbowski* Court characterized her dispute with the HMO as one involving denial of benefits rather than as a decision touching on medical treatment. The court therefore followed a line of precedent finding preemption (most of it preceding the U.S. Supreme Court's June 2000 decision in *Pegram v. Herdrich*) rather than the line of precedent finding no preemption where the HMO is accused of making decisions that adversely affect the quality of health care rather than eligibility for care (the "quantity" of care, in the words of some courts).

> The rationale for these holdings (finding preemption) is that the decision whether a requested benefit or service is covered by the ERISA plan falls within the scope of the administrative responsibilities of the HMO or insurance company, and is therefore "related to" the employee benefits plan.
>
> *   *   *
>
> In contrast, claims challenging the quality of care are not preempted (by ERISA).

245 F.3d at 278-79.

Reading *Pappas* and *Pryzbowski* together creates more than a little impression of inconsistency among the courts. Pappas allegedly suffered injury because of a 3- to 4-hour delay in obtaining HMO approval for surgery in a conflict over whether the HMO would pay for treatment at a particular facility by particular physicians. Pryzbowski allegedly suffered injury because of a 6- to 7-month delay in obtaining HMO approval for surgery in a conflict over whether the HMO would pay for treatment at a particular facility by particular physicians. One would expect the cases to either both be preempted by ERISA or neither be preempted by ERISA. Although one can attempt to differentiate the facts to harmonize the results of these two cases, this is an exercise in legal cleverness more than an adequate explanation. The Pennsylvania Supreme Court and the Third Circuit simply have taken different views as to what constitutes "plan administration" and a "mixed" question of medical treatment. So, too, will other cases until a majority rule emerges or the Supreme Court again intervenes.

My view is that the *Pappas* Court has made the correct post-*Pegram* analysis. HMO authorization decisions that involve a decision about the necessity for out-of-network treatment or the most appropriate facility for treatment are usually inherently mixed decisions of medicine and administration because they turn in part on determining whether medical treatment imperatives justify treatment outside the HMO network. The better reading of *Pegram* is that these types of decisions sound more in medical negligence than plan administration and should not be preempted by ERISA. *Pappas* is correct. *Pryzbowski* is wrong.

Recall that in *Pryzbowski*, there was no question that the patient was a covered member of the HMO plan. The question was whether her afflictions justified the recommended treatment by out-of-network physicians. In making this determination, the typical HMO decides based on the nature of the medical situation and the relative wisdom of using in-network or out-of-network doctors and hospitals. There is no question that the patient, under the appropriate circumstances, is entitled to out-of-network care, usually based on whether the medical condition demands it. In other words, HMOs of necessity decide the out-of-network question based in part on the HMO's assessment of the medical situation. Under *Pegram*, this is a mixed question (or possibly even a pure medical treatment question), and ERISA preemption should not apply. After *Pegram*, ERISA preempts claims of plan administration error against an HMO only when the HMO's decision is one based solely on contract without consideration of medical issues presented by the patient's case. Unfortunately, *Pryzbowski* may indicate that many courts are continuing to be overprotective of HMOs notwithstanding *Pegram*[1] and other cases since 1995 that have lowered ERISA's preemptive shield for health care plans.

HMOs operating under a *Pappas* regime rather than a *Pryzbowski* regime are not defenseless. If the *Pryzbowski* case against the HMO had been permitted to continue, U.S. Healthcare would have been entitled to raise a number of defenses, including (i) the delay was not a cause of the continued back pain; (ii) the surgery was the problem; (iii) the out-of-network doctor (who now is 0 for 2 in curing Pryzbowski's back problems) was at fault or recommended continued treatment by his team without sufficient medical justification); and (iv) in-network doctors were perfectly competent to perform the surgery, and Pryzbowski's insistence on use of out-of-network doctors is what caused the delay.

---

[1] Or perhaps because of *Pegram*. Although *Pegram*'s holding logically suggests limited preemption by ERISA, *Pegram* 's rhetoric is very laudatory of the HMO concept of health care rationing and reflects concern that liability claims not undermine the economic feasibility of these types of health care plans.

Although the HMO would undoubtedly prefer not to defend these claims at all, many would argue that HMOs should be required to defend delays or refusals concerning out-of-network care when the patient has a nonfrivolous argument that the delay was unwarranted and caused injury. ERISA was enacted as a pension benefit regulation to protect workers; it was not enacted as an immunity law for health care plans.

A lingering post-*Pegram* ERISA question is whether a decision of pure plan administration might be subject to the fiduciary duty obligations of ERISA, which are normally imposed on the plan, on the non-health care plan administrator, and on entities that handle the funds of an employer-provided benefits plan. *Pegram* clearly stated that HMOs and others that make medical or mixed treatment decisions are not acting as fiduciaries. But if the HMO is acting only to administer a plan, does it not resemble closely a bank holding plan assets or an employer determining who may obtain benefits? After *Pryzbowski*, lawyers making claims against an HMO may be inclined to plead both nonfiduciary claims (in hope that the court adopts a *Pappas* analysis) and fiduciary claims (in hope of attempting to succeed in a fiduciary duty claim if the court rejects the medical negligence claim on *Pryzbowski*-like grounds). But *see Batas v. Prudential Ins. Co.*, 281 A.D.2d 260, 724 N.Y.Supp. 2d 3 (1st Dept.—March 20, 2001) (refusing to permit state law-based breach of fiduciary duty action against health plan; health insurer is not a fiduciary).

The juxtaposition of *Pappas* and *Pryzbowski* reveals the continuing judicial uncertainty over the parameters of ERISA preemption. The U.S. Supreme Court has granted certiorari to review the decision in *Moran v. Rush Prudential HMO, Inc.*, 230 F.3d 959 (7th Cir. 2000), in which the federal appeals court in Chicago upheld (on a 2-1 vote) an Illinois statute requiring independent medical review of HMO denials of treatment. *See* 121 S.Ct. 2589 (June 29, 2001). Oral argument was heard in October 2001. The Court may use the *Moran* case not only to decide questions of state regulation but also to clarify the law of ERISA preemption in general. Commentators reviewing the *Pegram* decision have uniformly seen it reducing the quasi-immunity of HMOs that is provided by ERISA preemption.

The Court may use the upcoming *Moran* opinion to more clearly affirm or deny this interpretation of *Pegram* and to choose between the *Pappas* and *Pryzbowski* approaches to ERISA preemption of medical treatment decisions.

ARSON EXCLUSION VIOLATED STATUTE AND PUBLIC POLICY WHEN APPLIED TO INNOCENT COINSURED

Lane v. Security Mutual Insurance Co., 96 N.Y.2d 1, 747 N.E.2d 1270, 724 N.Y.S.2d 670 (New York Court of Appeals—February 13, 2001)

Security Mutual issued a homeowner's policy to Joretta Lane that contained an exclusion for losses arising out of an intentional fire set by an "insured." The term included not only the named insured but also relatives living at home.

> While the policy was in effect, the plaintiff's 17-year-old son intentionally set the premises on fire. Although the plaintiff's son was solely respon-

sible for the arson, the defendant disclaimed liability based on the policy exclusion for intentional acts by "an insured."

747 N.E.2d at 1271.

The court of Appeals, New York's highest court, held the exclusion unenforceable as against Lane, who had nothing to do with her son's arson activity.

> We hold that the subject exclusion impermissibility restricts the coverage mandated by statute and afforded the innocent insured. The New York standard fire insurance policy is codified in [New York] Insurance Law §3404(e). Any policy that insures against the peril of fire must incorporate "terms and provisions no less favorable to the insured than those contained in the standard policy." The standard policy exclusion provision entitled "Conditions suspending or restricting insurance" states that damages will be disclaimed "for loss occurring *** while the hazard is increased by any means within the control or knowledge of the insured." The standard policy is the minimum level of coverage permissible for an insurance company to issue.

747 N.E.2d at 1271.

The court found that a child's arson was not the result of hazard increase within the parent's control. Because Insurance Law §3404 "delineates independent liabilities and obligations as to each insured to refrain from incendiary acts," the court found it at odds with the statutes—as well as concerns of fairness and equity—that the policy attempted to strip an innocent insured of coverage. 747 N.E.2d at 1272.

The Court of Appeals opinion, although short, reads like a brief against the arson exclusion, or any exclusion punishing nonculpable policyholders. To some extent, a policyholder purchases insurance to protect not only against the negligence of household members and the outside world but also against the occasional unpredictable antisocial behavior of the members of the household. But the court stopped well short of gutting these types of exclusions across the board, holding that its decision in *Lane* "is limited to matters involving fire insurance, where Insurance Law §3404 is implicated." For liability insurance, exclusions taking coverage from all policyholders because of the wrongdoing of a single insured are apparently permissible in New York. *See* 747 N.E.2d at 1272; *Allstate Insurance Co. v. Mugavero*, 79 N.Y.2d 153, 589 N.E.2d 365, 581 N.Y.S.2d 142 (1992).

WORKERS' COMPENSATION COVERS PSYCHIATRIC INJURY; NO NEED FOR PHYSICAL MANIFESTATIONS OR IMPACT ACCOMPANYING PSYCHIC LOSS

Bailey v. Republic Engineered Steels, Inc., 91 Ohio St. 3d 38; 741 N.E.2d 121 (Ohio Supreme Court—February 7, 2001)

Leonard Bailey was operating a tow motor when he accidentally ran over and killed a coworker at Republic Engineered Steels. Bailey became severely depressed as a result of the accident and required treatment. When he sought compensation pursuant to Ohio's workers' compensation law, he was denied at all administrative levels.

The relevant statutory section states that a compensable injury "does not include . . . [p]sychiatric conditions except where the conditions have arisen from an injury or occupational disease." *See* Ohio R.C. 4123.01(C)(1).

The Bureau of Workers' Compensation took the view that Bailey had not sustained a compensable injury as required by statute. When Bailey continued to attempt to obtain benefits, the trial court also rebuffed him. However, the intermediate court of appeals was more receptive, finding for Bailey but with a resolve uncertain enough to certify the issue for Ohio Supreme Court review. The Ohio Supreme Court clarified the reach of workers' compensation benefits when it held that "a psychiatric condition of an employee arising from a compensable injury or occupational disease suffered by a third person is compensable" under the law.

> The plain reading of the statute reveals that the intent of the General Assembly is to limit claims for psychiatric conditions to situations in which the conditions arise from an injury or occupational disease. However, [the statute] does not specify who must be injured or who must sustain an occupational disease.

91 Ohio St. 3d at 40, 741 N.E.2d at 123.

After reviewing the history, theory, and purpose of workers' compensation laws (where strict liability is imposed but benefits are limited in a compromise between labor and management interests), the court concluded that the statute must be construed in favor of the claimant and at least not construed so as to add limitations on recovery that are not in the text of the statute.

The dissenters argued that the statute and the system were designed to compensate only the worker tangibly injured on the job. *See* 91 Ohio St. at 42; 741 N.E.2d at 125. However, the dissent does not really refute one notion at the core of the majority holding: Bailey was in fact injured in a workplace mishap; he did not develop his affliction off-site merely as a result of knowledge of a coworker's injury. Bailey was at the center of the injury and probably blamed himself for the tragedy as well. He was completely immersed in a deadly workplace mishap. As the majority reasoned, the fact that his injuries were mental rather than physical would not appear to deprive him of coverage.

Undoubtedly, employers reading a case like *Bailey* are concerned that the pool of compensable workers not expand too dramatically once the "lid" is off the topic of psychic injury. For example, it would seem too much if scores of workers could claim compensation merely upon hearing of an unknown coworker's death in another sector of a large manufacturing plant. But Bailey's claim was much more concrete and directly related to his role as a worker. Although cases falling between these extremes will present difficult characterization problems, courts should not have difficulty placing situations like Bailey's in the category of compensable claims and differentiating this from more attenuated or outlandish claims for compensation out of coworker sympathy.

SECURITY GUARD'S HEART ATTACK AFTER CONFRONTATION WITH HOOLIGANS IS COVERED "ACCIDENT" UNDER STATE WORKERS' COMPENSATION SCHEME

Cunningham v. Shelton Security Service, Inc., 46 S.W.3d 131 (Tennessee Supreme Court—March 1, 2001) (rehearing denied, May 2, 2001)

Robert Cunningham worked as a security guard at the Little Barn Deli and Market in Nashville. During the early morning hours of March 5, 1992, three young men entered the store and apparently attempted to shoplift. Cunningham confronted the men and asked them to leave. A verbal confrontation ensued and things became heated, but violence did not erupt as Cunningham escorted the three men out of the store, although they threatened to return and kill Cunningham.

When Cunningham returned to the store, he soon began complaining about feeling bad. He rubbed his arm and stated that he had a funny sensation. He went outside for a moment and fell unconscious, the victim of a heart attack. Cunningham died before his ambulance reached the hospital. An emergency room physician attributed the tragedy to "sudden cardiac death," which he attributed to the distressing nature of the confrontation. However, Cunningham's death certificate classified the death as one from "arteriosclerotic cardiovascular disease," and no autopsy was performed.

The legal issue before the court was whether Cunningham's death was the result of an "injury by accident arising out of and in the course of employment"as required by the state workers' compensation statute. *See* Tenn. Code Ann. §50-6-102(12) (1999). The court, reasoning from the statutory language and precedent, found that the death was sufficiently work-related and accidental to qualify for coverage. "[T]he injury must result from a danger or hazard peculiar to the work or be caused by a risk inherent in the nature of the work." The court found that the Cunningham injury substantially originated at work and was linked to work in time and space.

> [T]he rule is settled in this jurisdiction that physical or mental injuries caused by worry, anxiety, or emotional stress of a general nature or ordinary stress associated with the worker's occupation are not compensable. The injury must have resulted from an incident of abnormal and unusual stressful proportions, rather than the day-to-day mental stresses and tension to which to workers in that field are occasionally subjected.

> [T]he record also reflects that the individuals chased off by the employee threatened to return and kill him. We believe that this additional circumstance makes a difference and is sufficient to warrant the conclusion that the employee's death did not result from generalized employment conditions, but from something beyond the norm, even for a security guard.

46 S.W.3d at 137.

FEDERAL APPEALS COURT HOLDS THAT CALIFORNIA HOLOCAUST VICTIM INSURANCE RELIEF ACT OF 1999 DOES NOT VIOLATE COMMERCE CLAUSE OF U.S. CONSTITUTION OR FEDERAL GOVERNMENT'S FOREIGN AFFAIRS POWER

Gerling Global Reinsurance Corp. of America. v. Low, 240 F.3d 739 (U.S. Court of Appeals for the Ninth Circuit—February 7, 2001)

In the late 1990s, a long-slumbering issue of history and insurance emerged. Facts brought to light tended to confirm long-standing suspicions that European insurers had opportunistically seized upon the ravages of World War II and the Nazi Holocaust against the Jews to avoid paying life insurance benefits to the beneficiaries of Jewish decedents killed during the war years. State insurance commissioners held hearings and often heard poignant stories of families losing the benefit of policies on which years of premiums had been paid.

The insurers had long argued that they could not pay benefits without documentation or other very solid proof of the existence of the claimed policies. Investigation suggested that the insurer archives knew more than the insurers had been telling. Personal testimony by survivors was credited as establishing the likely existence of policies even if the exact terms and limits were not available.

Claimants and insurers were both faced with severe problems of proof and proportionality. Protracted litigation was unlikely to benefit either side. The National Association of Insurance Commissioners (NAIC) and various state legislatures enacted NAIC-proposed model legislation designed to require insurers to provide information on policies in effect between 1920 and 1945 as a condition of remaining in good standing to do business in California. Under the statute, if a company fails to comply, the Insurance Commissioner is required to suspend the insurer's certificate of authority.

Three insurers and an industry trade organization challenged the law and sought a preliminary injunction, arguing that the Holocaust Victim Insurance Relief Act of 1999 (HVIRA) violated the Commerce Clause and the foreign affairs power of the U.S. Constitution by interfering too greatly with the interstate flow of goods and the international relations of the federal government.

The trial court granted the preliminary injunction. The U.S. Court of Appeals for the Ninth Circuit (which includes California, Oregon, Washington, Idaho, Montana, Nevada, Arizona, and New Mexico) left the injunction in place but reversed the trial court's assessment of the Commerce Clause and foreign affairs power issues. The injunction was not vacated, so that the insurers could present to the trial court the question of whether the provisions of HVIRA might violate the due process of rights of the insurers.

In reaching its decision, the Ninth Circuit found that the McCarran-Ferguson Act applied and made the dormant Commerce Clause of the Constitution inapplicable. The "dormant" Commerce Clause power prevents states from taking actions that inhibit interstate commerce. Congress uses "active" Commerce Clause power when it enacts legislation regulating states and other entities based on the Commerce Clause power. The McCarran-Ferguson Act provides, in quite strong terminology, that insurance is largely to be regulated by the states. Consequently, state insurance regulation, even if based on investigation for wrongdoing and with commerce-limiting potential penalties, was not inconsistent with the Commerce Clause and the federal structure.

As to the ability to conduct foreign affairs, which normally resides in the executive branch of the national government, Congress has in fact passed the U.S. Holocaust Assets Commission Act of 1998 (22 U.S.C. §1621) to facilitate investigation of the matter and location of as many of the lost insurance policy assets as possible. Under these circumstances, there was no state usurpation of foreign policy power: "We read the Holocaust Act to embrace state legislation like HVIRA." *See* 240 F.3d at 748.

Thus, the Ninth Circuit reversed the trial court on the merits but did not dissolve the injunction. The appellate court was concerned that there may be insufficient due process if California was seeking to impose liability on insurers without sufficient contact between the state and the objects of the regulation. For that reason, no attempt was made to remove the injunction, and the case was remanded to the trial court for consideration of the due process claim.

Insurance Company Held Liable for $6 Million and Interest Plus $6 Million in Plaintiff's Counsel Fees for Violating Fiduciary Duties Under ERISA

Harris Trust and Savings Bank v. John Hancock Mutual Life Ins. Co., 122 F. Supp. 2d 444 (U.S. District Court for the Southern District of New York—November 22, 2000) *Harris Trust and Savings Bank v. John Hancock Mutual Life Ins. Co.*, 2001 U.S. Dist. LEXIS 3649 (U.S. District Court for the Southern District of New York—March 31, 2001)

An employer benefits plan begun in 1941 became the subject of a long-running dispute between the plan trustee and an insurance company holding some of its assets. In essence, insurer John Hancock held funds for investment as part of the retirement plan for the Sperry Rand Corporation (SRC), which later became Unisys. For a number of years, the trust was able to obtain funds held in excess of those required to meet plan obligations in what then was referred to as a "rollover procedure."

In 1982, the SRC attempted again to use the rollover procedure to withdraw accumulated free funds, but Hancock refused to let the SRC do so, citing its own cash flow needs. The SRC then attempted to withdraw accumulated free funds to pay nonguaranteed benefits, but Hancock provided notice that it would no longer pay nonguaranteed benefits under the agreement previously applied. As a consequence of Hancock's refusals to permit such access to "free funds," the only mechanism available for the SRC to withdraw free funds was the transfer provisions of GAC 50. Again, however, that was not a viable option because of the pricing scheme (which controlled such transactions based on low interest rate assumptions made decades earlier).

Hancock did not consider its obligations under ERISA to the plan when it decided to terminate the rollover procedure or the payment of nonguaranteed benefits with excess funds. Instead, it used plan assets for its own benefit: to help address its own cash flow problems, as "one more way of limiting cash outflows." In addition, by refusing to permit the withdrawal of free funds, Hancock was able to continue collecting charges on the investment income generated by these funds. There was no question that the free funds belonged to the trust; the issues confronting the parties were how to compute the amount of the excess funds, when Hancock had to give them back, and under what circumstances.

Throughout this period, Hancock assessed the trust risk charges. However, Hancock did not actually face any risk with respect to the free funds during this time period because it was "sufficiently protected" by other provisions of GAC 50 so that it was not at "material risk." Therefore, the excess risk charges collected by Hancock during this time period constituted overcompensation. 122 F.Supp.2d at 452 (citations to trial record omitted).

The court concluded that Hancock "violated its obligations [as a fiduciary] under ERISA by breaching its duty of loyalty and its duty to avoid prohibited transactions." 122 F. Supp. 2d at 459. According to the court:

> Hancock refused to return Plan assets to the Trust when the Trust sought to use the rollover procedure in 1982 to withdraw accumulated free funds. The Trust felt it could get a better return by investing the excess funds elsewhere, but Hancock refused to return the Plan assets because of its cash flow problems. Instead, Hancock exercised its discretion to terminate the rollover procedures that had enabled the Trust to withdraw a total of $12 million prior to 1982. Clearly, Hancock put its own interests and cash flow needs ahead of the interests of the Plan and its beneficiaries. By doing so, Hancock violated its obligations under ERISA.

> Hancock also refused to revalue the liabilities on a fair and reasonable basis. It repeatedly recognized that because of outdated interest and mortality assumptions, the liabilities [of one group annuity investment contract] were grossly overstated . . . . Hancock had the discretion to revalue the LOF but exercised its discretion in a manner that furthered its own interests and disadvantaged the interest of the Plan.

122 F. Supp. 2d at 459-60.

The court rejected Hancock's argument that its status as a mutual insurer required it to give equal consideration to its other contract holders and thus use funds to alleviate its cash flow problem rather than release funds to SRC as requested. *See* 122 F. Supp. 2d at 462. In addition, the Court suggested that Hancock's argument was pretextual because "Hancock has maintained for years that ERISA did not apply and that it was not a fiduciary under ERISA." 122 F. Supp. 2d at 462. Hancock had aggressively defended the litigation since its inception in 1983, including taking the ERISA and fiduciary duty questions to the U.S. Supreme Court, where the Trust prevailed. *See John Hancock Mut. Life Ins. Co. v. Harris Trust and Savings Bank*, 510 U.S. 86, 114 S.Ct. 517, 126 L.Ed. 2d 524 (1993) (holding that funds held by Hancock were assets of the SRC plan and that Hancock's management actions were to be judged by the fiduciary standards in ERISA).

In its opinion imposing liability on Hancock, the court concluded that the economic loss to the Sperry Trust, with interest, was approximately $20 million. The court also ruled that the trust was entitled to an award of counsel fees. ERISA provides that prevailing parties are ordinarily entitled to a payment of reasonable counsel fees by the losing party. The court, in its November 22, 2000, opinion instructed the parties to make submissions on the issue of the appropriate amount of fees. In its March 30, 2001, opinion, the court awarded more than $6 million ($6,365,384.85, to be precise) to plaintiff's counsel (the law firm of Anderson, Kill, and Olick). Although the amount of fees was high, the court found the award merited by the considerable effort expended by counsel and the favorable results obtained. As the court noted, the group annuity contract at issue had been entered into during 1941, requiring counsel to investigate "facts spanning five decades." In addition to the thick motion practice, appeals, and trip to the Supreme Court, there were 51 depositions taken in the case, "thousands of exhibits," and a 13-day trial. *See* 2001 U.S. Dist. LEXIS 3649 at *7.

The court found the rates of counsel to be reasonable and focused particularly on the hourly billing rate of plaintiff's lead counsel Lawrence Kill, whose billing rate began at $210 per hour (in 1984) and gradually increased to $500 by December 2000. Although the rate was high, the court found it in line with the standards of New York City law firms and justified by the quality of the representation as well as the result (a judgment of approximately $20 million, when interest was included). "In this extremely complicated and difficult case, the work of Mr. Kill and his colleagues was superb." *Id.* at *15.

Hancock undoubtedly will prosecute an appeal with the same vigor its counsel has shown throughout the case. It will be most interesting to see if the compensatory award and the award of counsel fees are upheld. Even if there is reduction—or even reversal—*Harris Trust v. John Hancock* should serve as a cautionary note to entities that administer ERISA plan assets. They are likely to be considered fiduciaries in their handling of plan assets. As fiduciaries, they are required to display loyalty to the plan and to put the plan's interest ahead of their own. According to the court, Hancock failed to do this by essentially "playing the float" of the time value of money in Hancock's own favor rather than that of a client who specifically requested Hancock's help in reaping this benefit of the plan's own funds.

BOOK REVIEWS

Social Security Pensions: Development and Reform, by Colin Gillion, John Turner, Clive Bailey, and Denis Latulippe, 2000, Geneva: International Labour Office

Reviewer: Vickie L. Bajtelsmit, Colorado State University

This book represents a remarkable accomplishment for its editors and authors in that it compiles in one (admittedly daunting, 700-page) volume such a wealth of data, theory, and useful recommendations for scholars of Social Security pensions around the world. The editors have brought together the thinking of dozens of pension researchers from around the world and compiled them in a thoughtful and well-organized text. Whether the reader is a pension economist, a public policy maker involved in pension reform, or merely an interested observer, the extensive factual review of many countries' successes and failures and the practicalities of running a pension scheme are sure to add value.

The book is organized in four sections. The first section, consisting of 14 chapters, provides a broad overview of the structure and design of public pension programs and their problems. This includes excellent coverage of the design of benefits, options for financing benefits, and the management of investments. At the end of this section, the authors include several chapters addressing some of the specific economic concerns that are at the heart of Social Security reform in many developed countries today: demographic shifts, inter- and intragenerational redistribution, and labor market effects. They conclude the first section with a chapter addressing public finance and accounting issues.

Part II is focused on the reform of Social Security pensions and can be considered to be the heart and soul of this book, as it sets the tone for all that comes before and after. Having identified the necessity for reform, the six chapters in this section recommend some normative guidelines for reform and outline policy options. As such, these are perhaps the most controversial and most interesting chapters. A course in pension economics would benefit from having its students delve into the issues raised here as a platform for an informed debate. The recommendations, and indeed the flavor of the entire book, are heavily weighted toward principles that have been established for many years by the International Labour Office in Geneva, the sponsor of this project. These principles include universal participation and coverage as well as cost-of-living adjustments of benefits that replace at least 40 percent of preretirement earnings.

The third section of the book is a collection of six regional briefs that summarize issues and concerns in specific areas of the world, including Asia and the Pacific,

Africa, Latin America and the Caribbean, the Middle East, Central and Eastern Europe, and the OECD countries. Each brief provides an overview of the economic and socioeconomic environment and an explanation of the existing pension environment and reforms on the horizon, if any. These are admittedly thumbnail sketches of complex environments, but they illustrate many of the issues that are addressed elsewhere in the book.

The last section, composed of "technical briefs," provides a variety of information, models, and data relating to pension coverage, governance, and reform. The statistical section includes numerous tables comparing countries on different variables important to the central issues covered in the book: demographics, age and participation conditions needed to qualify for public pension benefits, coverage ratios, sources of retirement income, public expenditures on Social Security benefits and administration, and legal provisions on contributions and financing.

I strongly recommend this book for anyone teaching or researching in the pensions area. It is a must-read for Ph.D. students who are interested in these topics, as it provides an excellent overview of the issues as well as an extensive bibliography for further research.

Workers' Compensation: Benefits, Costs and Safety Under Alternative Insurance Arrangements, by Terry Thomason, Timothy P. Schmidle, and John F. Burton Jr., 2001, Kalamazoo, Michigan: W. E. Upjohn Institute for Employment Research

Reviewer: John D. Worrall, Rutgers University

This book succeeds on many fronts and is a must-buy for those working in social insurance, human resources, or public policy. The careful construction of a cross-sectional time series on the costs of workers' compensation alone would be a major contribution and worth the price of the book, facilitating research on the changing structure of workers' compensation programs. However, the book actually uses the series to examine the adequacy, equity, and efficiency of the workers' compensation system. The authors update previous studies, Krueger and Burton (1990) and Schmidle (1994), for example, and they price both the essential recommendations of the National Commission on State Workmen's Compensation Laws and the Model Act of the Council of State Governments. They consider public vs. private provision and the injury prevention role of workers' compensation programs.

Those familiar with the research programs of the three authors, all experienced scholars who have made many contributions to social insurance research, will see the influence each has had on the final product. Although each is interested in theory and econometrics, the authors go to great pains to make the book accessible to the general reader. They explain technical points in good English and clearly spell out the public policy aspects of the research.

After a brief overview (Chapter 1), the authors present an especially well-written Chapter 2 on workers' compensation program developments since the 1960s. This will provide a quick review for those who have followed workers' compensation programs closely and a strong basis for the research to come for those unfamiliar with workers' compensation research. Chapter 3 provides the data foundation for the multivariate statistical research that follows in Chapters 4, 5, 7, and 8 (Chapter 6 sets out the theory and reviews the effect of rate regulation).

The authors provide detailed information on the construction of their cross-sectional time series. They are able to build a consistent series for workers' compensation class codes, which account for approximately 75 percent of premium. This is careful and laborious research, and it is essential for empirical work. Chapter 4 is devoted to basic cost regressions and the ultimate issue of the trade off between adequacy and affordability. The authors found that the simple imposition of the Model Act could increase the average costs of workers' compensation by 60 to 75 percent! Chapter 5 takes up system efficiency and the public vs. private provision issue. This is an area fraught with measurement problems (hidden costs in the public system, for example) and small sample sizes, but the authors do a good job with the data that they have. Chapter 7 examines the impact of rate regulation on workers' compensation costs. The major findings of the chapter are that partial deregulation is associated with higher employer cost, and more extensive deregulation with lower employer cost. Chapter 8 considers the impact of insurance arrangements on workplace safety. The authors find that exclusive state funds are associated with higher accident rates, but competitive state funds correspond to lower accident rates. Chapter 9 sets out the findings and policy implications.

Some scholars may have minor quibbles with this book: We probably do not observe real employer costs (employers engage in wage trade offs with employees); we do not have 100 percent compensation class code compatibility or coverage; we do not observe insurance prices exactly (or the timing of cash flows at the firm level), which can make regulation studies problematic. The authors are aware of these pitfalls and make the best use of the data set they have constructed. That set is the best constructed to date, and this book will be a contender for several book of the year awards.

REFERENCES

Krueger, A. B., and J. F. Burton Jr., 1990, The Employers' Cost of Workers' Compensation Insurance: Magnitudes, Determinants and Public Policy, *Review of Economics and Statistics* 72(2): 228-240.

Schmidle, T. P., 1994, The Impact of Insurance Pricing on the Employers' Cost of Workers' Compensation Insurance, Ph.D. dissertation, Cornell University.

Automobile Insurance: Road Safety, New Drivers, Risks, Insurance Fraud and Regulation, edited by Georges Dionne and Claire Laberge-Nadeau, 1999, Dordrecht, The Netherlands: Kluwer Academic Publishers

Reviewer: Richard A. Derrig, Automobile Insurers Bureau of Massachusetts

This volume is one of five categorizing the many topics examined in 1996 on the occasion of the 25th anniversary of the Center for Research on Transportation (CRT) at the University of Montreal. The editors have organized an intriguing melange of papers that speak to current and important issues for automobile insurance in North America. The central theme, however, is controlling the social cost of automobile accidents. Insurance pricing, fraud, inexperienced drivers, and regulatory effects are the four elements of (insured) accident costs covered by 31 authors of the 22 papers in the book.

This reviewer will not compete with the excellent six-page summary of the papers by the editors. Rather, the two short rearrangements of topics and results listed below are meant to entice the reader to run, not walk, to the nearest library or bookstore, obtain a copy of the book, and peruse the papers.

Accidents. Inexperience, risky behavior, dangerous roads, alcohol, and medical conditions of commercial drivers each work to increase accidents. Innovative restricted or "graduated" licensing plans for new and youthful drivers, statistical methods to evaluate effective driver training programs and hazardous road sites, alcohol involvement as a multistage decision problem, and isolation of truck drivers with serious medical conditions are all covered in a search for lower accident involvement.

Costs. The asymmetry of both *ex ante* insurability and *ex post* claiming information provides for a wide variation in auto accident costs. Adverse selection arising from inefficient insurance contracts and rating methods, increased discretionary or "excess" claims that accompany perverse economic incentives in the variety of tort systems, and the direct and indirect costs of claim fraud all tend to increase the total cost of the auto accident insurance system. Contract redesign and operational strategies, reduction of fraud-inducing incentives by law or regulation (no fault, "no pay, no play," and the Quebec model are the examples studied), and aggressive investigation of suspected fraud are explored with enlightening results.

The great variety of topics and points of view in this volume will enhance the ability to "pick and choose" those inquiries that appeal to your academic or personal interests. It is as though the Montreal Expos played the New York Yankees at home and were allowed to position 31 all-stars in the field—an entertaining experience for all the Montreal (CRT) fans!

The Fair Value of Insurance Business, edited by Irwin T. Vanderhoof and Edward I. Altman, 2000, New York: Kluwer Academic Publishers

Reviewer: J. Paul Newsome, Lehman Brothers, New York City

In May 2001, approximately 120 financial analysts and portfolio managers from some of the largest investment complexes in the country attended the "Lehman Brothers' Insurance University" Conference to learn about analysis and accounting for insurance companies. The conference, and the relatively large number of investors who attended a conference with an otherwise esoteric topic, underscored how confusing insurance accounting can be and the importance of appropriately valuing insurance businesses. So while *The Fair Value of Insurance Business* is the published results of a conference held in March 1999, it is fair to say that the topic remains of great interest to practitioners.

The book can also be viewed as one step in a longer journey that accounting and financial analytical theorists are taking for insurance companies. Today, insurance accounting remains the last bastion of accrual accounting—where insurance revenues are dutifully matched with insurance expenses over the lifetime of the insurance policies. The method, of course, depends upon the type of contract, but insurance accounting stands in contrast to much of modern accounting that focuses more on the balance sheet. Currently, the principal accounting governing bodies—the FASB and the international accounting board—are discussing changing the accounting for insurance companies to more appropriately value assets and liabilities. Under GAAP today, the balance sheet of the typical insurance company is treated in a lopsided way. Assets are largely market-to-market, but liabilities are largely booked at what could be called "historic cost." Efforts are afoot to change the accounting for insurance companies so that both sides of the balance sheet are market-to-market—so-called fair-value accounting.

The Fair Value of Insurance Business provides a number of building blocks for the theory and practice of fair-value accounting as well as examples of how a fair-value method might be accomplished.

The book is divided into three sections. "The Intellectual Underpinnings" begins with a chapter written by Luke N. Girard that reconciles a key issue that was unresolved by a similar conference that preceded the 1999 conference from whence the book came. Is the direct method or the appraisal method to calculating insurance liabilities more appropriate? The answer, Girard demonstrates, is that both methods will arrive at the same answer so long as the underlying assumptions agree. The second half of this section is left to a chapter by Sam Gutterman that discusses the selection of a discounting interest rate needed for fair-value calculations.

The "Elaboration of Theory" section contains three chapters by Thomas S. Y. Ho, Martha Wallace, and Mary Lynn Michel. The first two of these chapters take the basic theory discussed in the first section and propose more robust methods for using the basic theory to value insurance liabilities. Michel's chapter bridges the gap between the "elaboration of theory" and the next chapter, which discusses more concrete examples of how fair-value accounting might work by discussing the role of earnings, reported book value, and fair-value disclosures on the valuation of stock companies.

The "Illustrations of Fair-Value Calculations" section ends the book with two chapters by J. Peter Duran and R. Thomas Herget that provide examples of the effect of fair-valuing annuity contracts and term insurance.

Contrary to what this reviewer thought before finishing the book, the book will appeal to a much wider audience than the academic-looking cover would suggest. Once past Girard's highly mathematical chapter, the book discusses a wide variety of topics that would appeal to insurance accountants, investment professionals at insurance companies, and insurance investors besides actuaries and insurance academics. For example, Michel's chapter, "Earnings, Historical-Cost Book Values, and Fair-Value Disclosures in the Valuation of Stock Life Insurance Companies," was helpful in work I do as an industry-sector equity analyst for Lehman Brothers. The book should appeal to those practitioners and theorists who want to better improve their understanding of how fair-value accounting methods can work.

Managing Environmental Risk Through Insurance, by Paul H. Freeman and Howard Kunreuther, 1997, Boston: Kluwer Academic Publishers

Reviewer: William L. Ferguson, The University of Louisiana at Lafayette

Managing Environmental Risk Through Insurance is the ninth publication in the Kluwer series "Studies in Risk and Uncertainty," edited by Professor W. Kip Viscusi. Authors Freeman and Kunreuther (FK) provide an excellent addition to the series, exploring the issue of whether private insurance can "be used as a means to obtain compliance with governmental environmental policy" (vii). Although targeted primarily at policymakers, the book is clearly written and may prove useful to insurance academics as either a required or supplemental reading in a collegiate risk/insurance seminar.

FK present their analysis in two sections, the first dealing with managing societal risks in general, and the second with managing certain environmental risks.

The first section opens with three chapters comparing the management of societal risks through governmental benefits programs, the tort legal system, and insurance. In the first chapter, FK offer insights into various governmental programs (for example, low-interest disaster relief loans, federal subsidy of repairs to public structures and infrastructure, state guaranty funds). They provide a balanced, compelling assessment in laying out key elements of their analysis. For example, FK postulate that the essential characteristic of governmental programs is the understandable tendency to emphasize equity over efficiency, without regard to need. Thus, government programs tend to encourage certain (undesirable) behaviors by focusing simply on a claimant's eligibility for benefits rather than "whether the claimant should have avoided [the event] in the first place" (8). FK observe that the primary advantage that such governmental focus on post-event benefits qualification has over pre-event planning is that lower unit administrative costs typically accrue in the benefits disbursement process. Yet FK clearly recognize the primary weaknesses of such government programs: "They do nothing to lower the risk and likelihood of loss, and they subsidize certain individuals and businesses at the expense of all taxpayers" (10).

The second chapter examines the system of incentives inherent in tort law and presents a brief history of key environmental legislation in the United States governing clean water (1972), air (1977), and soil (through the Resource Conservation and Recovery Act [1976], CERCLA [1980], and EPA underground storage tank [UST] regulations). FK state that the "polluter pays" principle of strict liability, which was created through governmental shifting of responsibility for risk onto those perceived to have created it, was expected (incorrectly) by scholars to better spread risk and encourage loss control. FK thus present a strong case that the primary limitations of the tort system are in identifying actual causal links between exposure and injury, as well as the extraordinarily high transaction costs that reduce funding efficiency for remediation and cleanup.

The third chapter discusses the historical significance of insurance in general, the specific features of insurance that make insurance attractive for managing societal risks, the role of reinsurance in creating markets, and the transaction costs associated with using insurance as a policy tool. The key features of insurance identified by FK include risk spreading, variance reduction in predicted frequency and severity of loss in setting reserves, segregation and categorization of risks to reduce cross-subsidization, the encouragement of loss control, the value of outside monitoring and inspection of insureds by insurers, and the role of reinsurance to further spread risk. The chapter closes with a brief discussion of payment capacity and transaction costs for general liability insurance and environmental claims. Although "asbestos and CERCLA liabilities are distinctly different" (28), FK state that the applicable transaction costs are of roughly the same magnitude (that is, with only approximately 40 percent of claims costs going to plaintiffs), based on certain RAND and American Academy of Actuaries studies of such claims. However, these tort liability claims are still relatively inefficient in contrast to traditional situations, "when insurance exists for specific liabilities" where "[g]enerally, liability insurance pays 66 percent of allocated premiums to claimants" (29). Thus, FK argue that "insurance appears to be a promising alternative to the current practice of dealing with environmental risks solely through the tort liability system" (30).

The second section of the book begins with a brief overview of the basic insurability and marketability requirements necessary for the successful development of private risk transfer mechanisms. The fourth chapter identifies the two primary conditions for insurability as identifying and quantifying the exposure so as to be able to set premiums for specific risks. FK use the availability of data regarding relative frequency and severity of fire, earthquake, and underground storage tank losses to explain the identification process. They go on to discuss the importance of the ambiguity of risk and the problems of adverse selection, moral hazard, and correlated risk, as well as administrative loading, in setting potential premiums. FK then use the case of a hypothetical closely held commercial manufacturer of safer underground storage tanks to illustrate their proposed process of developing a break-even premium curve as a function of demand.

The fifth chapter employs another case-type example, this time using the problem of friable asbestos. This chapter provides a fair amount of detail identifying various aspects of the regulatory process specific to the risk of leaving asbestos in place or engaging in abatement. The sixth chapter addresses the issue of insurability and marketability of the asbestos risk. Given well-specified federal regulations, mandates, and standards of behavior regarding asbestos, FK state that it may yet be possible to develop and analyze credible data regarding the probability and magnitude of fiber exposure levels. FK explain further that minimal potential problems with adverse selection, moral hazard, and risk correlation may be encountered in setting an adequate minimum pure premium. Anticipated demand from motivated contractors, coupled to a lesser extent with incentives for building owners concerned about asbestos, lead FK to propose that the asbestos risk should ultimately prove both insurable and marketable.

In Chapter 7, FK employ their analytical framework to evaluate potential insurability and marketability for three other important environmental risks: property owner liability for contaminated property, UST leakage, and lead-based paint abatement. With regard to contaminated property liability, FK review the history and limited success of property transfer liability coverage since it was introduced in 1992. FK note that, in contrast to asbestos and despite generating significant pre-existing loss data, encouraging identification of existing contamination exposures, and remediation, contaminated property liability coverage has been driven largely by due diligence site assessments imposed by financial lenders or credit agencies rather than as a broad component of environmental risk management. In the case of USTs, FK frame the failure of private market initiatives squarely in a traditional asset-substitution argument: The existence of flat fee/taxed state guaranty funds trades post-loss remedies for pre-loss prevention. Finally, the failure of lead-based paint abatement coverage is shown to suffer from a lack of explicit regulatory guidelines regarding exposure levels, which has negatively affected the insurability of such losses rather than their marketability. These three cases lead FK to suggest what heretofore may have been an unpopular and politically unlikely eventuality: that "the development of government regulation ought to take into account the needs of private insurers to develop and market new products" (96). This may, or may not, occur as insurers seek new growth opportunities in the wake of market pressures exacerbated by the recent World Trade Center disaster.

Taking the book as a whole, Freeman and Kunreuther offer a thorough and thoughtful discussion of the key strengths and weaknesses of using insurance as a social policy tool. Their book makes a solid contribution to policymakers, insurance academics, and students interested in the formulation and assessment of strategies designed to deal with certain, necessarily well-defined, environmental risks.

CALL FOR PAPERS

29th Seminar of the European Group of Risk and Insurance Economists

Nottingham, September 16-18, 2002

The 29th Seminar of the European Group of Risk and Insurance Economists will take place in Nottingham on September 16-18, 2002. Professors **Stephen Diacon** (Stephen.Diacon@nottingham.ac.uk) and Richard MacMinn are the local organizers.

Papers can be on any topic of Economics, Finance or Management Science as related to risk and insurance.

On the occasion of the seminar, the 2002 Geneva Risk Economics Lecture will be delivered by **Hans-Werner Sinn (U. of Munich)** on:

« Weber's Law and the Biological Evolution of Risk Preferences »

Chairmen of the scientific program are Roland Eisen and Achim Wambach. Papers should be submitted by April 15, 2002 to Eisen@wiwi.uni-frankfurt.de or in hardcopy to Prof. Roland Eisen, Department of Economics, University of Frankfurt, D-60054 Frankfurt am Main, Germany.

The seminar is sponsored by the Geneva Association.

A selection of papers from the seminar will be invited for publication in *The Geneva Papers on Risk and Insurance Theory.*

Call for Papers
Announcement of $6,000 in Research Awards

The **Advanta Center for Financial Services Studies** at **Temple University's Fox School of Business and Management,** in partnership with the **American Risk and Insurance Association**, is pleased to announce a call for papers in the area of

Financial Services Security.

Qualifying submissions will be eligible for the following research awards:

- 1 prize of $3,000 for the best paper overall, and
- 2 prizes of $1,500 each for the next best papers in each of two sub-categories (described below),

to be funded by the Advanta Center at Temple.

All prize-winning papers will be published in a special symposium issue of the *Risk Management and Insurance Review* (a journal of the American Risk and Insurance Association).[1] Non-prize-winning papers may also be considered for publication.

Through this awards program, Temple's Advanta Center hopes to stimulate interest in research related to security issues associated with the financial services sector in the post-September 11, 2001 world. Topics may fall into either of two categories:

(1) the general security concerns of financial services firms and their customers (e.g., the security of computer systems, electronic fund transfers, and e-banking with respect to both the physical integrity and confidentiality of electronic systems), or

(2) the national security concerns of governments as they relate to the financial activities of, and funding of, terrorist organizations and states (e.g., the use of financial systems such as international banks and *hawaleh* for illicit fund transfers, money-laundering, and the raising and distribution of capital).

By making submissions, authors implicitly affirm that their work is original, has not been published in any other forum, and is/will not be reviewed simultaneously by another forum without the consent of the organizers of this program.

Please submit all inquiries and papers by e-mail attachment to:
Michael R. Powers, Director
Advanta Center for Financial Services Studies
The Fox School
Temple University
<michael.powers@temple.edu>.

Submission deadline: July 31, 2002. Prizes to be announced: September 30, 2002.

---

[1] The Advanta Center reserves the right not to make awards—and the *Risk Management and Insurance Review* reserves the right not to publish—if submissions are deemed to be of insufficient quality.

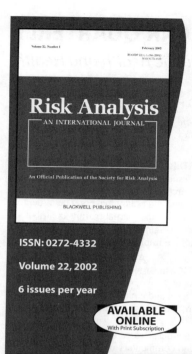

THE
MILBANK
QUARTERLY

A JOURNAL OF

PUBLIC HEALTH

AND HEALTH

CARE POLICY

Volume 79
Number 4, 2001

PUBLISHED BY
THE MILBANK MEMORIAL FUND
SINCE 1925

Blackwell Publishers
Boston, MA Oxford, UK

ISSN: 0887-378X

Volume 80, 2002

4 issues per year

AVAILABLE ONLINE
With Print Subscription

THE MILBANK QUARTERLY

A Journal of Public Health and Health Care Policy

Editor: BRADFORD H. GRAY

*Ranked the **Number One** journal by impact factor in the category of Health Policy & Services in ISI's 2000 Journal Citation Reports!*

THE MILBANK QUARTERLY is devoted to scholarly analysis of significant issues in health and health care policy. It presents original research, policy analysis, and commentary from academics, clinicians, and policy makers. The in-depth, multidisciplinary approach of the journal permits contributors to explore fully the social origins of health in our society and to examine in detail the implications of different health policies.

Topics addressed in **THE MILBANK QUARTERLY** include the impact of social factors on health, prevention, allocation of health care resources, legal and ethical issues in health policy, hospital administration, and the organization and financing of health care.

You'll find outstanding articles, research notes, policy review and analysis, and commentary on health and health care policy.

Published on behalf of the *Milbank Memorial Fund*.

SAMPLE CONTENTS

SELECT - Blackwell Publishing Email Updates   *Select*

You can now receive the tables of contents of *The Milbank Quarterly* emailed directly to your desktop. Uniquely flexible, SELECT allows you to choose exactly the information you need. For FREE updates on *The Milbank Quarterly* and other Blackwell Publishing titles simply visit:

http://select.blackwellpublishers.co.uk

Blackwell Publishing

Call **1-800-835-6770** *(toll free in N. America)*
or: +1 781-388-8206 (US Office); +44 1865 244083 (UK office)
subscrip@blackwellpub.com
www.blackwellpub.com

View a FREE Online Sample Issue

www.blackwellpublishers.co.uk/journals/milq